Shedding Light on
HIS DARK
MATERIALS

KURT BRUNER
JIM WARE

AN IMPRINT OF TYNDALE HOUSE PUBLISHERS, INC.

Visit Tyndale's exciting Web site at www.tyndale.com

TYNDALE is a registered trademark of Tyndale House Publishers, Inc.

SaltRiver and the SaltRiver logo are registered trademarks of Tyndale House Publishers, Inc.

Shedding Light on His Dark Materials: Exploring Hidden Spiritual Themes in Philip Pullman's Popular Series

Copyright © 2007 by Kurt Bruner and Jim Ware. All rights reserved.

Cover photo of compass copyright © by Emrah Turudu/iStockphoto. All rights reserved.

Author photo of Jim Ware copyright © 2003 by Tom Sluder Photography. All rights reserved.

Designed by Jessie McGrath

Published in association with the literary agency of Alive Communications, Inc., 7680 Goddard Street, Suite 200, Colorado Springs, CO 80920.

All Scripture quotations, unless otherwise indicated, are taken from the New King James Version®. Copyright © 1982 by Thomas Nelson, Inc. Used by permission. All rights reserved.

Scripture quotations marked NIV are taken from the HOLY BIBLE, NEW INTERNATIONAL VERSION®. NIV®. Copyright © 1973, 1978, 1984 by International Bible Society. Used by permission of Zondervan. All rights reserved.

Scripture quotations marked NASB are taken from the *New American Standard Bible®*, © 1960, 1962, 1963, 1968, 1971, 1972, 1973, 1975, 1977, 1995 by The Lockman Foundation. Used by permission.

Scripture quotations marked KJV are taken from the *Holy Bible*, King James Version.

Scripture quotations marked ESV are from *The Holy Bible*, English Standard Version®, copyright © 2001 by Crossway Bibles, a publishing ministry of Good News Publishers. Used by permission. All rights reserved.

Library of Congress Cataloging-in-Publication Data

Bruner, Kurt D.
   Shedding light on His dark materials : exploring hidden spiritual themes in Philip Pullman's popular series / Kurt Bruner and Jim Ware.
      p. cm.
   Includes bibliographical references (p.   ).
   ISBN-13: 978-1-4143-1564-5
   ISBN-10: 1-4143-1564-3
   1. Pullman, Philip, date. His dark materials. 2. Christianity in literature. 3. Apologetics. 4. Fantasy fiction, English—History and criticism. 5. Young adult fiction, English—History and criticism. I. Ware, Jim. II. Title.
   PR6066.U44Z57 2007
   823'.914--dc22   2007017424

Printed in the United States of America

13   12   11   10   09   08   07
7   6   5   4   3   2   1

*To all who seek liberation
from the tyrant of self.*

Table of Contents

Introduction

As one madly in love with the writings of J. R. R. Tolkien and C. S. Lewis, I suppose I had no choice in the matter. Upon hearing of Philip Pullman's *His Dark Materials* series, I knew it would join *The Lord of the Rings* and *The Chronicles of Narnia* on my list of mandatory reading. I hoped to discover yet another writer capable of immersing my imagination in spiritual themes by whisking me off to other worlds. As our earlier Finding God books have shown, fairy stories carry us away to places our more sensible inclinations might avoid. In the process, we are caught off guard by truths we've known our entire lives—even to the point of boredom—with an infusion of surprise and wonder.

As I read Pullman's series, I was not disappointed. He clearly has the gift and knows how to weave spiritual themes into the fabric of a well-told tale. And yet I don't remember when an author's work has left me more disturbed.

Like his fantasy-genre predecessors Tolkien and Lewis, Philip Pullman lives in Oxford, England. Although he has never achieved the scholarly merits or academic status of either man, he did teach part-time for several years at Oxford's Westminster College before dedicating himself to writing full-time. So while only on the fringe of the academy, Pullman's imagination has flourished in the city many consider the capital of fantasy literature. And it shows. His brilliant craftsmanship betrays a love for some of the most influential British authors of all time.

Like the men who gave us Bilbo Baggins and Queen Lucy, Pullman has written books that have sold millions and millions of copies. In fact, they have emerged as one of the most widely read fantasy series produced in the past decade, trailing only Harry Potter in popularity among adolescent readers. Pullman's books are so popular, in fact, that New Line Cinema chose *His Dark Materials* as its first major fantasy film series to follow Peter Jackson's blockbuster trilogy *The Lord of the Rings*.

Similar to the writings of Tolkien and Lewis, *His Dark Materials* is carried along by profoundly spiritual undercurrents that, at times, overpower plot and character. It would be difficult to read his series without tripping over Pullman's overtly religious agenda, which, in my mind, was where the similarities between Pullman and his famous Oxford ancestors end and my concern over his growing influence began.

As we examined in *Finding God in The Lord of the Rings* and *Finding God in The Hobbit*, J. R. R. Tolkien's Middle-earth is a world that bubbles up from solidly Christian theology. Masterfully subtle in his approach, Tolkien pioneered a genre of literature that allows the author to carry readers on to a stage where themes such as good over evil and heroic self-sacrifice can be encountered. By no means trite or cute, the world of Tolkien contains disturbing images and oppressive shadows. But in the end, light breaks through in what he called "eucatastrophe," thrilling our hearts as the bright surprise of redemption overtakes the ominous cloud of darkness. Millions of readers have enjoyed themes rooted in Tolkien's Christian faith, though most of them have no idea of the true source of their pleasure.

C. S. Lewis also used fairy stories to help readers encounter God, most notably in his seven *Chronicles of Narnia* tales. Inspired by the writings of his predecessor George MacDonald and influenced by his love of ancient mythology, Lewis used an approach similar to Tolkien's—though much more overt. While the Narnia stories are not allegory, they do grow out of a central supposition. *Suppose* there existed another world, peopled by animals rather than human beings. *Suppose* that world fell, like ours, and had in it someone who was the equivalent of Christ. Aslan entered Narnia in the form of a lion just as Jesus came into this world in the form of a man.

Based upon this notion, Lewis created a fantasy world that depicts the central theme of our real world—redemption through the incarnate God's death and resurrection. As we explained in *Finding God in the Land of Narnia*, the magical part is that this mythical Christ somehow draws us closer to the Real Christ. Why? Because, as Lewis would say, a fantasy tale has none of the "stained glass and Sunday school associations" that diminish one's sense of wonder.

So Philip Pullman stands in good company in using the

genre of fantasy literature to carry spiritual themes. His inventive brilliance rivals that of J. R. R. Tolkien and J. K. Rowling, who are also master storytellers and creators of other worlds. Why, then, did I find his series so disturbing? Because, unlike Tolkien's works of Christian imagination or Rowling's relatively innocent fun, many of Pullman's spiritual undercurrents run in direct opposition to the God of Christianity.

Some have gone so far as to call Pullman "the most dangerous author in Britain"[1] because his trilogy presents a universe in which rebellion against a tyrannical "Authority" is encouraged, the church is depicted as an oppressive institution that suppresses truth and freedom, and "his dark materials" (a concept borrowed from Milton's *Paradise Lost*, regarding Satan's rebellion) open our eyes to the "truth" that we came into existence out of our own energy rather than being created by some illegitimate, decrepit deity.

Despite Pullman's obvious vitriol against the orthodox Christian faith, however, some believers find themselves agreeing with many of his characterizations and attacks against the organized church. In some ways, the "God" he seeks to murder deserves to die. The question we must ask, however, is whether his plot ultimately targets Jehovah Himself.

If it does, what are we to make of the hints of a familiar moral center within the series? For, as we will explore throughout this book, Pullman can't entirely get away from a spirituality he seems eager to escape, due to a "spiritual impulse" he both acknowledges and shares.

> The religious impulse [is one] which I would characterize as the impulse to feel awe, wonder, a sense of mystery, a sense of delight in being alive, and in being a part of this great, extraordinary universe. That I can't gainsay and I wouldn't gainsay because that's something that I feel myself. It's a very important part of what makes us human beings; this sense of wonder and delight and mystery.[2]

Truer words have never been spoken. Our sense of wonder, delight, and mystery attest to our humanity—the very part of us most connected to God because it reflects His image—*Imago Dei*. That's why Pullman's "spiritual impulse" has compelled him to offer unwitting tribute to the very God his work intended to attack.

A person only casts a shadow when standing near the lamp. Pullman may have turned his back to the light, choosing to see only the extended form of his own dark shadow. But the story he tells strongly suggests the existence of an illuminating bulb we Christians know as the light of the world. A light, says the apostle John, that "shines in the darkness, and the darkness has not overcome it" (John 1:4-5, esv).

One reason Jim and I chose to write this book is to help

parents navigate the *His Dark Materials* cultural buzz certain to engulf their children when the stories make it to the big screen. As with the Harry Potter phenomenon, nearly every child will likely want to devour these books as the stories' characters hit movie screens and Happy Meals. Moms and dads need to understand the initially latent but eventually overt attacks against the foundations of Christian belief beneath the core story line. To that end, we hope this brief overview proves helpful.

But we also intend to treat Pullman's series with the respect it deserves as well-crafted art containing much beauty. Our book tries to help readers reflect on rather than replace experiencing Pullman's own works. To this end, we begin each essay with an imaginative paraphrasing of a scene from *His Dark Materials*, followed by our thoughts on its significance to the underlying spiritual themes of the series. We consider not just Pullman's troubling agenda, but the often inspiring inference of an imagination engulfed by the very light it can't bring itself to face. An imagination that touches truths the author himself might wish to reject.

In that spirit, we invite you to join us as we seek to discover the light behind the shadows cast in *His Dark Materials*.

Kurt Bruner

OTHER WORLDS

Lyra's anxiety rose as her view from the wardrobe became obstructed. The Master, arriving late for the meeting, blocked the otherwise perfect view she'd created by leaving the doors slightly ajar. Fortunately, he moved away from the gap before calling his fellow scholars to attention. The time had come for Lord Asriel's presentation.

The room had been off-limits to children, especially girls. But to Lyra it was just another forbidden corner of the university campus to explore. When she'd heard approaching footsteps, she'd decided to hide in the wardrobe and spy. As Lyra pushed the collection of soft and prickly coats aside, she had no idea that her latest adventure would pull her into worlds she didn't know existed.

I

So far, no one seemed aware of her hidden attendance. No one, that is, except for Lord Asriel. But Lyra had saved his life moments earlier by alerting him to the poison in his drink, so he welcomed her nosy alliance as he presented his most recent findings to his academic benefactors, at least one of whom wanted him dead. Lyra sat stealthily watching and listening, hoping to pick up unwitting confessions from the whispered conversations of those seated near the wardrobe. Like her own, each of their daemons seemed to betray feelings of intimidation and jealousy at Asriel's dominating presence. Clearly, he was a very important and powerful man.

As part of his talk, Lord Asriel showed several slides. And what mysterious slides they were; photogramic images like none Lyra or anyone else in the room had ever seen.

The first slide showed a snow-covered hut on the distant horizon surrounded by various philosophical instruments, complete with aerials, wires, and insulators. In the foreground stood a man clad in heavy furs to protect him from a harsh, arctic cold. Beside the man stood a smaller figure, perhaps a child.

As he prepared to show the second slide, Lord Asriel explained that this image of the same scene had been taken one minute later with a specially prepared emulsion.

The image changed drastically, the man now bathed in a brilliant light.

His hand was raised, and glowing particles seemed to flow from his fingers.

"What is that light?" asked the Chaplain.

But it wasn't light. As Lord Asriel's punch line clarified, "It is Dust."

A sudden and ominous silence immediately overtook the room, and Lyra sensed that he meant something more significant than ordinary dust with a small *d*. Moments later the room filled with exclamations of surprise.

Lord Asriel replaced the slide with another, also taken at night, containing a small group of tents and travel gear resting beneath the Aurora, or Northern Lights.

Again, Asriel replaced the traditional slide with one containing the same scene moments later using his special photogram technique—revealing an even more mysterious and troubling image.

Peering more intently through the tiny gap, Lyra could see within the illumined sky the unmistakable outline of buildings, towers, and streets. A city! Suppressing a gasp of wonder, she listened to equally amazed reactions from beyond the wardrobe doors.

All of the Scholars noticed the city. It couldn't be missed. Some seemed to show a reserved giddiness, as if they were seeing a living, breathing specimen of a creature long assumed merely mythical. Others reacted with skepticism, even disapproval.

KURT BRUNER and JIM WARE

The conversation continued, but Lyra understood very little. She drifted off to sleep and was awakened by Lord Asriel after the others had departed. She could hardly contain her excitement, eager to discover more about what she had heard. But Lord Asriel seemed uninterested in expanding her education, ordering her to keep what she knew to herself and announcing he would be leaving shortly to go back to the North and continue his work.

Despite his pronouncements that he would go alone, Lyra begged to join him. "I want to find out about Dust. And that city in the air. Is it another world?"

* * * * *

Who among us hasn't longed for a chance to explore other worlds? As babies, our sense of wonder and curiosity kept our anxious mothers on their toes as we crawled toward whatever room remained uncharted. Lacking the developmental sophistication to do anything else, we popped most of the objects we discovered into our mouths in an attempt to taste our way to understanding. Every stairway, every table, every closet, and every container afforded an entirely new realm of learning.

The older we got, the further we traveled to scratch the itch for adventure. Human history includes a long tradition of exploration as we've edged our way further away from the tiresome and familiar to places where, in the words of *Star*

Trek's Captain Kirk, "no man has gone before." We've pushed the boundaries to find something new, something more. We risk life and limb to climb Mount Everest and build gigantic Apollo missiles to carry us to the moon. Our robots touch the bed of the Atlantic Ocean and analyze the floor of Mars.

And while our diligence and technology provide the leverage, they would be useless on our quest of discovery without that which gives them focus and purpose; something at the core of what it means to be human: imagination. Children pretended to be space travelers long before engineers designed the first rocket. Neil Armstrong's "giant leap" owes more to imagination than to science. The latter merely built what the former conceived.

Nothing has motivated our imaginings more than the desire for other worlds, be they around the corner, part of a mythical history, or through a wardrobe door. Few of us will ever have a chance to climb the world's tallest mountain or board NASA's next spacecraft. But millions of us can travel to new worlds through the power of the pen in the hand of great writers.

One of the greatest, J. R. R. Tolkien, wrote an essay describing the purpose and power of fantasy stories, a literary genre he introduced to twentieth-century readers—opening the door and creating an audience for those who would follow in his footsteps, including Philip Pullman.

"Fantasy is a natural human activity," wrote Tolkien. "It certainly does not destroy or even insult Reason; and it does not either blunt the appetite for, nor obscure the perception of, scientific verity. On the contrary. The keener and the clearer is the reason, the better fantasy will it make."[1]

Imagination is not the enemy of reason, but its lover. Both represent uniquely human capacities, gifts that allow us to discover realities beyond the obvious and mundane. "For creative Fantasy is founded upon the hard recognition that things are so in the world as it appears under the sun; on a recognition of fact, but not a slavery to it."[2]

So while reason enables us to calculate, decipher, and apply logic, imagination lets us conceive, explore, and invent.

Philip Pullman proves himself a master when it comes to conceiving other worlds worthy of the reader's exploration. Like genre predecessors Tolkien, Lewis, Madeleine L'Engle, and others, he seems a student of ancient poets who created mythical realms and heroic characters. But Pullman does something new. While he joins a great tradition of whisking readers off to imaginary lands filled with witches, daemons, angels, and other supernatural beings, Pullman's worlds also draw inspiration from cutting-edge scientific theory.

Throughout the three books, characters refer to a heretical doctrine suggesting the existence of many worlds. "Is this the Barnard-Stokes business?" a member of the Jordan College faculty asked Lord Asriel while looking at an inexplicable city in the sky. Everyone in the room knew what he meant. So can we.

The concept is based upon the Many-Worlds Interpretation of quantum mechanics. In layman's terms, it suggests that there are myriad worlds in the universe in addition to the one we know. In particular, every time something with potentially different outcomes occurs—such as a coin toss—one possibility becomes the reality in our world, while the other carries forward in another. In fact, Lord Asriel uses this very illustration to explain his research.

> Take the example of tossing a coin: it can come down heads or tails, and we don't know before it lands which way it's going to fall. If it comes down heads, that means that the possibility of its coming down tails has collapsed. Until that moment the two possibilities were equal.
>
> But on another world, it does come down tails. And when that happens, the two worlds split apart.[3]

So Lyra's world, while much like our own, contains traces of coins landing on the opposite side; for the most part, these are slight variations rather than fundamental differences. We have jet planes with pilots. In her world, air travel is in balloons navigated by aeronauts. Our Oxford has Queens College. Lyra's has Jordan College. We take pictures. They take photograms. And unlike our pictures, theirs never move. No wonder Lyra finds Will's local cinema a wonder.

While traveling from one world to the next with Lyra and the rest of Pullman's characters, readers experience a delicious combination of two rarely mixed ingredients—the wonder of fantasy and the mystery of science. In the process, however, Pullman comes close to diminishing some of the magic that more traditional fantasy literature engenders. That may be due to an internal tension every writer must resolve.

In his essay "Sometimes Fairy Stories May Say Best What's to Be Said," C. S. Lewis describes the conflict between a writer's "Author" and his "Man." The Author, driven by an unscratched itch and a desire to discover what might be, allows his story to unfold on its own momentum, unfettered by the practical, the profound, or the preferred. The Man, on the other hand, stands firmly grounded in the real world and his own philosophical predispositions, critical of the Author's work when it defies either. Subconsciously, the Man meddles with the Author's craft—turning a story that should affirm the soul's quest into something that forces an agenda. Good writers master both extremes, finding ways to allow both Author and Man to play their parts effectively. Fanciful stories lacking consistency won't ring true, but didactic sermons don't please the soul either.

His Dark Materials shows signs of this all-too-common tension. The world Pullman creates seems to vacillate between a latent desire for the God of Christianity and hostile criticism of the same. As subsequent chapters will show, the Man's philosophical agenda repeatedly spills onto the pages of the Author's work, leaving periodic stain marks on the dialogue of characters and on what becomes an upended moral center.

Tolkien warned of this possibility, suggesting fantasy "can, of course, be carried to excess. It can be ill done. It can be put to evil uses. It may even delude the minds out of which it came."[4]

On the whole, however, Pullman follows the best tradition of fantasy writers by satisfying his readers' yearning for the wonder of other worlds—worlds that allow us to explore new possibilities, encounter new creatures, and taste the mystery of what it means to be fully human. After all, since we were made in the image of the Creator, we are never more human than when we create.

LIGHT
Wonders of the imagination connect
us to the wonder of being human.

"Suppose your daemon settles in a shape you don't like?"

—*The Golden Compass*, Chapter 10,
"The Consul and the Bear"

DAEMONS

Peering over the ship's edge, Lyra strained to see what was creating such an exhilarating feeling. Pantalaimon couldn't be far away since daemons never ventured more than a short distance from their humans. He must have been swimming very near the hull.

Moments earlier, Pantalaimon had been joyfully skimming atop the waves as a petrel—his adventurous flight helping his human adjust to the seafaring life. Her second day aboard, Lyra understood too well the paralyzing effects of seasickness. But she began feeling better as her daemon tried several of the forms common to those who'd found their sea legs. His latest, a smooth and shiny dolphin, enabled him to join a school of the playful creatures as they leapt in gleeful refreshment below.

One of her new friends approached Lyra as she watched her bird-turned-dolphin companion. Now an adult with a settled seagull daemon, the seaman had once been in her place.

"Why must daemons settle?" she asked. Lyra wanted Pan to be able to change forms forever and resented the inevitable—when he would become fixed to a final form rather than enjoy the various adaptations he adopted as her situation or mood dictated.

"That's just the way it is." Not an explanation, but the only answer he had. He assured her she'd be glad when Pan replaced constant adaptation by assuming his fixed form. When Pan did, she'd know herself better.

Lyra couldn't believe it. She loved the unpredictability of an unsettled daemon. One moment Pan was a tiny, fluttering moth that made it impossible for anyone to read her emotions, the next a ferocious, snarling cat warning everyone to keep their distance. When she fell asleep, Pantalaimon curled up into his favorite resting form as a cute, cuddly mouse. Why would she ever want that to end?

The seaman told her about his daemon, Belisaria, who long before had settled as a seagull. Like the bird, the old seaman told her, he was hardy, able to find a bit of food, and good company wherever he happened to be. Lyra thought Belisaria suited him—not beautiful like a dove but a more tough and resourceful bird.

SHEDDING LIGHT
on *His Dark Materials*

In fact, every grownup she had ever met reflected his or her daemon's settled form. Or was it the other way round?

Mrs. Coulter, for example. Lyra remembered being so attracted to her at first—she was lovely, graceful, and superior. Her daemon, a perfectly groomed golden monkey, was equally striking and refined. But beneath the surface, both possessed a vicious, razor-sharp edge.

The Butler back at Jordan College, like all servants, had a dog that was eager to please and submissively tame.

John Faa, a man difficult to read beyond his air of strength and authority, had a crow—simple and commanding.

Lord Asriel, a man of great importance and intimidating stature, had a snow leopard, both stunning and fearsome.

Lyra had never been surprised by an adult's daemon; the connection between human persona and animal was always formfitting and unexceptional—as natural as one's eye color or height. Who they are is what you see—which is precisely why she disliked the idea of Pan settling. Why should others know so much about her at a glance? She worried, too, that Pan might settle in a shape she didn't like. What then?

The seaman acknowledged that some people were unhappy with their daemon. Yet eventually they had to accept what and who they are. As her friend got back to work, ending their conversation, Lyra glanced back at her carefree, ever-changing Pantalaimon. She decided she never *wanted to grow up.*

* * * * *

How does one really get to know other people? If you ask
them to tell you about themselves, they'll likely summarize
what they do: such as crunch numbers as an accountant, care
for children as a homemaker, see patients as a doctor, or
attend classes as a student. Using your skills of observation,
you can pick up additional clues. Do they wear expensive
clothes? If so, it could suggest either affluence or insecurity.
Do they seem self-effacing and deferential? That could suggest a meek temperament or a false humility. Do they carry
themselves confidently? That might mean they've successfully
overcome tremendous life obstacles or that they were raised
in privilege and never faced any obstacles.

Once we enter into a deeper relationship with a person,
truly knowing them comes in bits and pieces; the shape of the
smile, the tone of the voice, and the look in the eye all suggest
what he or she feels at any given moment. Such clues are too
small for most onlookers to notice, but they speak volumes
to the person eager to understand the meaning behind the
words and the person within the body.

The characters in Lyra's world have a tremendous advantage when it comes to getting to know another person, thanks
to a wonderful storytelling device that Philip Pullman considers his best creative idea—daemons.[1] Most readers would
agree. Not only do daemons help Lyra size up others at a

glance, but they also offer us unique insight into Pullman's view of the human experience.

When readers first come across the word in *His Dark Materials*, some might mistakenly assume these animal-formed beings are a misspelling of *demons*. Even Will, upon first meeting Lyra and learning of her daemon, made that mistake. "I don't know what you mean about demons," he said. "In my world *demon* means . . . it means devil, something evil."[2] But there is nothing deliberately demonic about daemons. They are nothing like the fallen angels coaxing humans toward hell like Wormwood in C. S. Lewis's *The Screwtape Letters*.

Others might try to compare daemons to those cartoon renditions of a miniature devil sitting on top of someone's shoulder opposite an angel on the other, each giving competing advice—an image often used to illustrate one's conscience and the continual battle between the temptation to sin and the admonition to be virtuous. This, also, misses the point of Pullman's daemon characters.

So, if not a devil or a conscience, what are these intriguing creatures?

The word *daemon* has a long and varied history, much of which certainly influenced Pullman's imagination. In the mythology of antiquity, daemons were an order of invisible personalities that the Romans considered mediating beings linking mankind to the gods. Greeks believed daemons to be lesser deities. Zeus assigned one daemon to each human at birth to attend, protect, and guide him or her through life and eventually death. Daemons were nameless, and like mankind, innumerable. Those that acted as personal attendants to higher deities took on particular forms and were given specific names.[3]

Plato referenced daemons in the *Apology* when Socrates explained that he resisted entering political life because something "divine and daemoniac" happened to him in which a voice "forbids something I am about to do, but never commands."[4] Possibly referring to one of those lesser gods Zeus might have assigned to him, Socrates experienced a protective influence from one who had no authority but did have tremendous sway on his decisions.

To Plato and his fellow ancients, daemons were considered creatures of a middle nature between gods and men—necessary to mediate between the two realms. This understanding of daemons continued as a central part of the medieval worldview, as when Milton, in *Paradise Lost*, refers to "Middle spirits—Betwixt the angelical and human kind" giving mortals intercourse with the gods.[5] Daemons were understood to have bodies, though more fragile and transparent than ours. Because they functioned in bodies rather than as pure spirit, Apuleius, a second-century student of Platonic philosophy, called them animals.[6]

Influenced by ancient and medieval writers including Plato and Milton, Philip Pullman seems to have borrowed their ideas to create animal companions for the humans of Lyra's world that serve as the bridge between each character's physical and spiritual self—more commonly called the soul. In fact, the bear Iorek Byrnison made the direct connection in a conversation about his lost armor. "A bear's armor is his soul, just as your daemon is your soul."[7]

Pullman uses daemons as anthropomorphic representations of the soul to portray profound and sometimes troubling insights about human dignity and individual personhood—most notably, our sex and sexuality.

First, daemons are almost always the opposite sex of their companions. Lyra, a female, has the male Pantalaimon. Lord Asriel, a male, has a female snow leopard. Watching the pairs interact replicates the experience of observing the intimate alliance of husband and wife—two become one. The connection reveals itself most intensely in those moments Lyra and Pan nearly lose each other, after which they desperately embrace like lovers reunited after long separation.

But the link to human sexuality becomes much more explicit in the taboo of touching another person's daemon. In *The Golden Compass*, for example, Lyra is assaulted by a group of men, one of whom, horror of horrors, handles her daemon. Pullman's description of the scene is meant to tighten one's stomach—as if one were reading an account of child molestation.

The men were gasping and grunting with pain or exertion, but they pulled and pulled.

And suddenly all the strength went out of her.

It was as if an alien hand had reached right inside where no hand had a right to be, and wrenched at something deep and precious.

She felt faint, dizzy, sick, disgusted, limp with shock.

One of the men was *holding* Pantalaimon. . .

She *felt* those hands. . . . It wasn't *allowed*. . . . Not *supposed* to touch . . . Wrong. . . .[8]

After the torturous incident, Mrs. Coulter reinforces the connection between one's daemon and one's sexuality by telling Lyra that daemons, while wonderful friends and companions when young, bring "troublesome thoughts and feelings" during and after puberty.[9] Hence, prepubescent daemons are free to change, while adult daemons "settle" into their permanent form.

In her essay "Second Nature: Daemons and Ideology in *The Golden Compass*," Maude Hines suggests that the natural connection between sexuality and identity is both represented and tested by the daemon's animal-ness—describing sexuality as animal urges and class hierarchies as animal taxonomies or classifications.[10]

The "class hierarchies" to which Hines refers show up

in *His Dark Materials* through the unspoken but clearly present class system that ranks one daemon (and its human) as higher than another. The Butler and other servants, for example, have dog daemons that willingly resign themselves to the superior rank and power of a snow leopard or golden monkey. It's just one more way a person's deepest identity and station in life show themselves in and through his or her daemon companion.

While his favorite and most striking imaginative invention, Pullman never clearly defines daemons—even allowing some contradictions to remain in their ways. (Daemons seem to alternate between one's alter ego, immortal soul, sexual impulse, and their Jiminy Cricket–like sidekick.) Still, he has created a literary device that connects readers to their deepest longings and reveals something fundamental about their deepest selves. We are more than merely physical beings. Each of us has, and each of us is, an immortal soul.

And the LORD God formed man of the dust of the ground, and breathed into his nostrils the breath of life; and man became a living being.
(GENESIS 2:7)

LIGHT

To be human is to be more than merely physical.

A human being with no daemon was like someone without a face, or with their ribs laid open and their heart torn out.

—*The Golden Compass*, CHAPTER 13, "FENCING"

"I AND THOU"

The man lowered his rifle and shuffled back toward the house, followed by his snarling wolverine daemon. Lyra trembled involuntarily as the door banged shut, dislodging a small avalanche of snow. Drawing the fur-lined hood of her anorak down around her face, she turned and asked Iorek Byrnison in a small, uncertain voice where she should go.

The great bear led her down to the edge of the frozen lake where a forlorn fish-drying hut stood on the icy shore, its plank walls gray with age, its tin roof thick with a layer of white. He stopped in front of the weather beaten door of the shed.

Hesitantly, she approached the rough wooden structure and laid a hand on the leather door latch. Two or three sharp yanks, and the door cracked open, swinging slowly outward on its hinges. Lyra bent and peered through the dim opening. It was terribly dark inside.

She wished she'd brought a lantern, though to tell the truth she was relieved that she couldn't see whatever it was that cowered in the shed. Whispering into Pan's fuzzy white ermine ear, she ordered him to become a bat and enter the shed first. But Pantalaimon, taking the form of a cat, wriggled out of her arms and jumped down into the snow, running back and forth in fear.

Steeling herself, Lyra drew a long, deep, icy breath. She stepped back and loudly ordered whoever was in the shed to come out.

Pantalaimon, panicked, sprang to her shoulder, pressing his furry side against her cheek.

She hesitated. Iorek stood several paces away, talking quietly with another one of the villagers, a fur-clad man who caught her eye and held a lantern aloft, swinging it in her direction. Heart pounding, mind racing, she hurried up the bank and took the dimly glowing object from his hand. Her sense of dread was like a lump of heavy ice in the pit of her stomach. Biting her lip, she returned to the shed, ducked under the lintel, and lifted the light.

In the corner, huddled against a rack of dried and frozen

fish, sat a little boy in a dingy, old anorak. His face was gaunt and pale. His eyes were round and staring. In his arms he cradled a piece of fish—stiff, lifeless, cold. He gazed up at her with an expression both pleading and uncomprehending. Lyra felt she was looking into the face of the living dead.

"Ratter," he said in a dull, flat voice. "You bring my Ratter?"

She caught her breath. A cold sweat broke out on her brow. The fine hairs stood up on the back of her neck. The boy had no daemon! No daemon at all! It was gone. Cut away. So this was what they called a *severed child*!

She felt she was going to retch. A violent sob forced its way up her throat. Clutching Pantalaimon to her breast, she squeezed her eyes shut and turned away.

* * * * *

Wholeness. Harmony. Togetherness. Peace. What the ancient Hebrews would have called *shalom*. In an important way, these words sum up what it means to be human in the fullest, most complete, most consummate sense of the term.

If you've ever experienced the absence of these qualities— *really* experienced it to the point of tears and anguish and searing pain; if you've ever known what it's like to be alone and alienated, shattered on the inside and broken on the outside, at odds with yourself and cut off from the rest of the world—then you'll understand the horror that confronted

Lyra when she peered into the little shed on the shore of the frozen lake.

In Lyra's world, as we've already discovered, everybody has a daemon, a kind of alter ego in animal form. A comforter, counselor, and constant companion. A living, breathing mirror of the inner self. Lyra's daemon is Pantalaimon—a name that some readers of Pullman's trilogy have interpreted to mean "all-merciful."[1] Together, a human being and his or her daemon constitute a whole person.

It's an effective narrative contrivance, this motif of the human–daemon relationship. From a purely dramatic standpoint it has the advantage of ensuring that the protagonist (Lyra) always has a congenial buddy or sidekick with whom to share thoughts and feelings and exciting experiences, an important element in any engaging adventure story. But the daemon is more than just a convenient literary gimmick. It's also a powerful image of a profound psychological and spiritual truth—a visual reminder that, at its deepest level, human life is meaningful only in terms of *I and Thou*.[2]

According to Christian theology, the universe revolves around a nucleus of *personality* and *relationship*. This is an assertion of profound significance and far-reaching implications. It stands opposed to every scheme that posits a purely material basis for the world in which we live. It gives the lie to all merely molecular explanations of the phenomenon of life. It assures us that the sense of *selfhood* that overshadows our day-to-day existence is not just an illusion, not just an anomaly, not just an inexplicable irregularity in the otherwise seamless fabric of a cold and voiceless universe.

We, like the One who made us, live according to the principle of *plurality* within *unity*. Each of us is a self-contained community. We exist in a state of constant dialogue with ourselves. As Jewish philosopher Martin Buber explains, "Self-perception and self-relationship are the peculiarly human, the irruption of a strange element into nature, the inner lot of man."[3] Self-awareness and self-knowledge—themes central to the message of *His Dark Materials*—arise out of this ongoing conversation between the inner and outer person. The poet John Donne expresses it this way:

> *I am a little world made cunningly*
> *Of Elements, and an Angelike spright*[4]

Down through the centuries, this bond between the "Elements" and the "Angelike spright" (angel-like spirit) has been represented in various ways. Some thinkers have spoken of a union between the spiritual and the physical. Others have used terms like *ego* and *id*. The subdivisions of *body*, *soul*, and *spirit* are familiar to anyone acquainted with traditional theological ideas about the nature of man. Pullman himself suggests a scheme of *body*, *daemon*, and *ghost*. However it is described and whatever name it bears, this intrapersonal dialogue, this circle of connectedness between the visible and invisible *I*, is basic to the human experience. It stands behind the notion of the conscience, which refers to knowledge shared with oneself (Romans 2:15).[5] It shows up in Paul's declaration that no one knows "the things of a man except the spirit of the man which is in him" (I Corinthians 2:11).

Pullman skillfully captures this fundamental truth for us in his invention of the daemon. The warmth and closeness of the human-daemon relationship bespeaks wholeness and health. A separation between the two is simply unthinkable. This is why a person without a daemon is an inconceivable terror: a nightmare so cruel and repulsive that even a "tough" kid like Lyra cannot bear to look upon it without sorrow and revulsion.

But look upon it she must; this is precisely the condition in which she finds little Tony Makarios, victim of the "child-cutters" of Bolvangar, who has taken refuge in a drying hut on the edge of a frozen lake in the far forsaken North. Severed from his daemon, Tony is reduced to an empty shell. In this state, he quickly fades and expires despite Lyra's desperate attempts to save him. "He couldn't settle," says Farder Coram, explaining the circumstances of Tony's death. "He couldn't stay in one place; he kept asking after his daemon, where she was, was she a coming soon, and all; . . . but he closed his eyes finally and fell still."[6]

From the biblical perspective, these primal principles of

personality and interrelationship are rooted in the nature of the Creator Himself. For God, while He is One, is also Three; and within the unity of the Godhead, the three persons of Father, Son, and Holy Spirit have been enjoying the sweet delights of communion and interpersonal fellowship from all eternity—the endless give and take of *I and Thou*.

Then God said, "Let Us make man in Our image, according to Our likeness." (GENESIS 1:26, NASB)

As persons made in the image of this triune God (Genesis 1:26), we human beings are designed to function in a similar pattern. Among other things, this means that we thrive best within the context of interaction with other people. Life, at its core, is all about *persons*, and persons, as Martin Buber declared, "appear by entering into relation to other persons."[7]

One thing seems clear: Philip Pullman knows that there is more to life than Dust and elementary particles. He understands that, apart from personality and relationship, both internal and external, human existence is devoid of significance. Through the vehicle of his story he helps us see that people are *not* just aggregates of shining, shimmering matter. He insists that human wholeness and harmony are functions of the mutual bond between the inner and outer self. As believers, we recognize that this bond is a reflection of the link between creature and Creator. In the scene narrated at the beginning of this chapter, Pullman paints a graphic and deeply affecting picture of what it means for little Tony Makarios to be cut off from his daemon, his soul—from the "I and Thou" that forms the basis of his own humanity. In the process, he gives us a powerful picture of what the Bible calls *sin* and *death*—the self-disintegration that is the direct result of man's alienation from the Ground of his being.

Ironic, isn't it? That, in Lyra's world, the villain behind this insidious plot to sever little children from their own souls should turn out to be *the Church*, the entity that, in *our* world, is entrusted with the message of wholeness and life. We'll want to return to this theme and examine it more closely in the pages that follow. But for now it's enough to note that the church is *supposed* to be an agent of divine healing and recon-ciliation, the living, breathing Body of Him who confronts each one of us with the poignant question: "What profit is it to a man if he gains the whole world, and loses his own soul?" (Matthew 16:26, NKJV).

Like Tony, we all know what it is like to be alienated and fragmented. We, too, are broken people: separated from God, from one another, and from ourselves by the power of sin and disobedience. Jesus, the Man who "gave up the ghost" on the cross (John 19:30, KJV), the Son who was cut off from His Father on the hill of Calvary (Mark 15:34), the Savior who suffered the pangs of separation and disintegration on our behalf—*He* is the One who offers us wholeness in exchange for the misery of our severed and unsettled existence. *He* is the One who supplies the *Thou* that answers to our *I*—who calls us by name and compels us to go forth and lead others into a life of reconciliation, unification, and inward peace: A life in which all may experience the joys of the eternal *I and Thou*.

He comes to us in our lonely darkness as Lyra came to Tony Makarios in his dreary little shed. He lifts a light at the door, looks us straight in the eye, and asks, "Do you want to be made whole?" (see John 5:6, KJV).

Everything depends on our answer.

LIGHT

Inward wholeness comes through
relationship with Christ alone.

DUST

Lyra and Pantalaimon clung to one another in desperate relief, overcome with emotion and trembling at the thought of what they had just experienced.

Those heartless, cruel men.

The sterile divider placed between Lyra and her beloved daemon.

The silver guillotine ready to cut them off from one another forever and ever.

Lyra had heard rumors of Gobblers for a long time. Everyone knew they kidnapped children. But few imagined what they did to them. And it had nearly happened to her. Her stomach tightened and sickened once again remembering poor Tony clinging desperately to a piece of fish after losing his daemon. Like him, she had been taken into the cutting room designed to sever children. And if not for the timely arrival of Mrs. Coulter, she would have shared Tony's terrible fate.

Mrs. Coulter, from whose London apartment Lyra had fled weeks earlier, now spoke comforting words while handing her a glass of chamomile. Yet Lyra knew better than to trust her. After all, Mrs. Coulter was one of them, perhaps even the mastermind behind the entire wicked operation. Her soothing words and gentle voice couldn't conceal the agenda Lyra knew was hiding beneath her questions about how Lyra had ended up here.

Pretending to have been kidnapped rather than having run away, Lyra wove together a string of what seemed plausible explanations for her sudden disappearance. But she had questions of her own. Why, she asked Mrs. Coulter, would anyone want to do the worst possible thing she could imagine: cut children off from their daemons?

"It's because of Dust, isn't it?" She demanded more than inquired.

Mrs. Coulter's voice assumed a patronizing and flavorless tone, as if parroting a dogma she had accepted rather than a truth she had found: Dust is bad, something wicked. The procedure was done for the children's own good, she assured Lyra.

Clearly, this was not the first time Mrs. Coulter had spoken those words. She, like nearly every other adult with whom Lyra had raised the topic, became anxious when discussing Dust—like children afraid of the Gobblers.

The Scholars back at Jordan College seemed unsettled when it came up during Lord Asriel's presentation.

Lord Boreal's reaction during Mrs. Coulter's cocktail party suggested more than mere curiosity. When Lyra mentioned to him learning about Rusakov Particles, the formal name given the Dust phenomenon, he seemed genuinely shocked that a young girl possessed such dangerous knowledge.

At the same party a man told the Bishop that Lord Asriel's experiments confirmed his belief that Dust emanates from the dark principle itself. She hadn't understood the phrase but knew anything called "dark principle" couldn't be good.

And then there was Serafina Pekkala's daemon, the majestic grey goose, who told Farder Coram that Dust came from the sky. While little was known about the Particles, the daemon said, adults would stop at nothing to discover more about it.

Stop at nothing indeed. Even if it meant sacrificing children!

Lyra returned to the moment as Mrs. Coulter continued her explanation that, since grown-ups and their daemons are already so infected with Dust, it was too late to help them.

Too late for what? What could be so terrible that cutting kids was considered "good" by comparison? It had to be a lie, even if Mrs. Coulter believed it herself. After all, she and every other adult had Dust, and they seemed perfectly fine. Could it really be so bad?

Lyra wanted desperately to escape, to take all of the other children with her, and to find Lord Asriel—the one adult who seemed unafraid. The one adult she could trust to tell her the truth about Dust.

*　*　*　*　*

Other than Lyra herself, nothing dominates Philip Pullman's *His Dark Materials* trilogy more than the idea of "Dust." It serves as the overarching mystery that must be solved and the central problem that must be overcome. It serves as the thread that holds the three books together, yet it proves the most elusive, even confusing, concept to grasp.

In Lyra's world, Dust is described as "a new kind of elementary particle," similar to atoms at one point while infused with "dark intentions, like the forms of thoughts not yet born" at others. Mrs. Coulter calls it something bad while Pantalaimon suggests it might be something good. In *The Subtle Knife*, in Dr. Malone's research lab based in our modern world, Dust is described as "dark matter" that comprises the bulk of the universe, but later in the story Dust introduces itself to her as "angels." Other possibilities include "physical evidence for original sin" and the dust from which Adam is said to have been created in the book of Genesis. So Dust vacillates between a microscopic particle of matter considered the basic universal building block and a spiritual entity with profound religious implications and intentions.

Pullman seems to have thrown a cacophony of sources into the stew of his imagination—a teaspoon of philosophy mixed with a pinch of religion and a dash of science, each contributing to the oddly varied flavor of Dust.

Let's begin with the scientific element. At the California Institute of Technology in 1933, Swiss astrophysicist Fritz Zwicky became the first to suggest the existence of a phenomenon that has come to be called dark matter. He inferred that the density of our universe requires the existence of about four hundred times more mass than can be seen. Therefore, there must be some nonvisible form of matter that provides enough mass and gravity to hold the orbiting galaxy clusters together.[1] As science writers Mary and John Gribbin explain, "Between 80 and 95 percent of the material of the Universe really is made of this stuff, which astronomers call non-baryonic Cold Dark Matter—or CDM, for short. This is the real science behind the Dark Materials in [Pullman's] trilogy."[2]

In *The Subtle Knife*, Dr. Mary Malone and her Oxford colleague Dr. Oliver Payne investigate the existence of dark matter, which they hypothesize to be some kind of elementary particle that is difficult to see. So they create a detector to filter out unwanted materials, amplifying the signal through a computer they've named the Cave. In this way they uncover the existence of shadow particles that appear to be conscious and are drawn to human consciousness. In this and other scenes, Pullman clearly draws upon the real-world phenomenon of dark matter that has been the focus of much cosmological research. Despite this loose connection, however, Dust seems more rooted in seventeenth-century philosophical speculation than twentieth-century science.

Baruch Spinoza began his brief forty-five-year life in 1633. He was born in Holland to Jewish parents who were living in exile away from their Portuguese homeland. Despite receiving a rabbinical education, in 1656 Spinoza was expelled from the synagogue in Amsterdam for defending heretical opinions, including his claim that he could demonstrate both the necessary existence and the unitary nature of a unique, single substance that comprises all of reality. Spinoza called the substance *Deus sive Natura* ("god or nature") and argued that it accounts for every feature of the universe. He described it as that which unites our spiritual and material beings and makes possible genuine human knowledge, which must be founded on the coordination of the spiritual and material realms.[3]

In other words, he deserted the traditional distinction between the spiritual and physical by suggesting that both spring from the same mysterious substance. Spinoza's philosophical speculation allowed him to abandon the transcendent God of Judaism and Christianity without ignoring mankind's spiritual impulse. He opened the door in monotheistic

Europe to a pantheistic worldview where God moves from benevolent Creator of everything to an impersonal synthesis of all.

Spinoza's opinions bear a strong resemblance to the dominant meaning Pullman gives Dust in his trilogy. His "elementary particles" seem to provide the foundation for a quasi-pantheistic convergence of spiritual mysteries and material stuff. As commentator Anne-Marie Bird explains:

> This, in effect, represents a rejection of one of the central ideologies underpinning Western modernity—that is, the desire to describe, categorize, and finally to segregate all that is ordered and rational from all that is chaotic or "other." The idea, in Pullman's scheme, is that each elementary particle consists of, or reflects different aspects of one and the same substance. In this sense, the texts reflect Spinoza's monistic doctrine that there exists one and only one substance: that is to say, the spiritual and the physical are simply two aspects of a single substance. . . .
>
> In Pullman's work, the suggestion is that Dust functions as a replacement for the redundant God. . . .
>
> Dust is a point of origin, a First Cause—a "presence" responsible for whatever else is "present"—in much the same way as the Christian God.[4]

In addition to the science of dark matter and the philosophy of Spinoza, Pullman also draws upon Christian thought as he adds ingredients to his creative stew. In fact, *The Golden Compass* opens with an ominous quotation from Book II of John Milton's *Paradise Lost*, which Pullman credits as one of his most important imaginative influences.

> *Into this wild abyss,*
> *The womb of nature and perhaps her grave,*
> *Of neither sea, nor shore, nor air, nor fire,*
> *But all these in their pregnant causes mixed*
> *Confusedly, and which thus must ever fight,*
> *Unless the almighty maker them ordain*
> *His dark materials to create more worlds . . .*[5]

In *Paradise Lost*, Milton listed the four elements (water, earth, air, and fire) that medieval minds considered the basic elements of creation—the "dark materials" with which the Almighty crafted all worlds in our cosmos. In *His Dark Materials*, Pullman goes much further by suggesting the existence of similarly foundational building blocks—"elementary particles" from which everything in both the physical and spiritual realms emerged. Lord Asriel even claimed these particles got their name from the Bible.

"Incidentally, the Bible gave us the name Dust as well," he told Lyra while turning to the book of Genesis.

> In the sweat of thy face shalt thou eat bread, till thou
> return unto the ground; for out of it wast thou taken:
> for dust thou art, and unto dust shalt thou return.
> (Genesis 3:19, KJV)

So Pullman agrees with Christians that man was formed from the dust of the ground. He just denies that the breath of God made man a living soul.

Even as Pullman empties such concepts of their Christian meaning, he uses them in the story to serve a larger agenda. For example, he links the idea of Dust to the doctrine of original sin in ways that become very important to the end of the story. Also, Pullman manages to create the impression in readers that cutting-edge science frightens religious leaders because it undermines their outdated, church-imposed assumptions.

But science has very little to do with the concept of Dust as Pullman expresses it. It is instead the product of a philosophical bias that many consider agenda. The author replaces the Christian grand narrative with one in which individual autonomy is the highest good. Instead of a transcendent God who created a distinct world, Pullman prefers a dark substance from which the heavens and the earth emerged.

The shadow cast by Pullman's concept of Dust reminds us of the grand narrative he, like Spinoza, has rejected. While at one time both men considered God the omniscient Author of our lives and of history, they ultimately decided He doesn't exist—which means no one can know the plot of the epic drama in which we find ourselves. As a whole, Western man has abandoned what philosophers call "metanarratives," eliminating hope of any overarching story that explains all of life. There are plenty of little stories competing for our allegiance—but no one big story that can capture our hearts or explain our lives.

Yet even our small stories shout an inescapable reality of the human spirit. We yearn for something transcendent, something bigger than ourselves to frame an otherwise meaningless existence.

Pullman's yearning led him to a mysteriously conscious substance, a dark soil from which everything sprouted to life.

For the Christian, the yearning affirms our deepest hopes and most reasonable expectations—that the soil in which we grow is tended by a caring, all powerful Gardener.

The Lord God planted a garden eastward in Eden, and there He put the man whom He had formed. (Genesis 2:8)

LIGHT

Life grows from soil tended by a loving Gardener.

> *"You en't human, Lord Asriel. You en't my father . . . Fathers are supposed to love their daughters, en't they?"*
>
> —*The Golden Compass*, CHAPTER 21, "LORD ASRIEL'S WELCOME"

FAMILY

Standing on the frozen tundra, Lyra strained to make out what was happening ahead. The frigid air seemed full of dark intentions, heavy with the presence of Dust as if a great and terrible event was about to unfold—about to bring her quest to some crashing conclusion.

Pantalaimon, in owl form for its nocturnal vision, landed on her wrist. He had spotted Lord Asriel and Roger just past the peak. He described the scene: Lord Asriel's snow leopard daemon had captured Roger's daemon in her mouth, so the boy couldn't escape. Lord Asriel was standing next to him beside instruments laid out in cruel anticipation.

Just then, all went dark—the brilliant glow of the Aurora flickering out like a dying anbaric bulb. Roger called out to Lyra in a panicked voice. She shouted back, promising a rescue she could not assure.

Lyra had set out on this quest in order to save Roger from the Gobblers, her efforts rewarded when she discovered him among the captured children back in Bolvanger. If she had taken much longer, he might have ended up on the cutting table, severed from his daemon like those other pitiful kids. But she had made it. He was safe. That is, until now. Lyra never imagined such a betrayal by the man she'd recently discovered was her father—the man she had trusted to do right by her and the others.

But he hadn't done right. He took Roger with him to the edge of the Northern Lights. And now she knew why. Lord Asriel planned to sever Roger, unleashing the tremendous jolt of energy needed to open the sky to that other world—the home of that city that had appeared in the photogram. As wicked and heartless as Mrs. Coulter, he too considered tortured children a small sacrifice on his way to possessing the power he craved.

Roger's desperate cries propelled her weakening legs through the blistering wind. She simply must reach him. She had promised to keep him safe.

Moments later, Lyra held Roger's limp body in her arms. Despite their heroic efforts, she and Pan had been unable to foil Asriel's well-planned intentions. Roger was dead, sacrificed on the cutting altar to please the god of ambition.

And of all people to carry out such a horrendous deed, her own father!

Lyra wished she had remained ignorant of his true identity. Why couldn't he have remained the distant, mysterious "Uncle Asriel" she saw infrequently during her years at Jordan College?

It seemed too much to absorb. Not so long ago, Lyra still had her identity as the half-tame, half-wild child roaming the halls and hidden rooms of Jordan's gothic campus, like the neighborhood cat everyone feeds and pets but nobody owns. Sure, the Master had general responsibility for her supervision, and she navigated the distant oversight of faculty and staff. But she pretty much lived the life of a free agent. Her mother and father had died when she was young. That's what they had told her. That's what she had believed.

Then the lovely Mrs. Coulter came on the scene, sweeping her away from the masculine realm of Jordan into a world of mysterious feminine charms. Oh, how Lyra had enjoyed being with her and how much she had wanted to be like her—at least until she saw beyond the exterior façade and perceived the calculating, manipulative woman underneath. But Mrs. Coulter was a liar. She not only knew about the Gobblers, she was their architect and commander—cutting children from their daemons.

So she had fled Mrs. Coulter in favor of her father. And when the gyptians explained her true identity, she felt a subconscious pride in her connection to so great a man as Lord Asriel. Now she wished that connection could be annulled.

She remembered how ungrateful he'd been to her back in the Svalbard prison where she had rescued him from his captors. "You don't love me, and I don't love you," she'd declared, adding, "I love an armored bear more than you, my own father!" Like everyone else, Lord Asriel viewed Lyra merely as a tool—an instrument for accomplishing his objective—and, if necessary, a sacrifice on his altar.

Now, standing near the opening through which her father had fled into another world, Lyra felt something new. Knowing the identity of her real parents, feeling the profound connection to their diabolical brilliance, she wished she could go back to being an orphan.

*   *   *   *   *

Few experiences are as painful to the ear as listening to an amateur musician butcher the notes of a well-written score. We cringe when a beginning violin player screeches through practice, a young pianist hits a flat instead of a sharp, or a junior-high trumpet player sours the final note of an otherwise perfect performance. A similar dissonance affects the spirit of someone raised without a loving family, like most of the children found in Philip Pullman's trilogy. They miss the intended melody as each endures the sour notes of family separation or estrangement.

Lyra is abandoned by her never-married father and mother to be raised as a "half-wild cat" on the campus of Jordan College. Once she learns the identity of her parents, she realizes they are anything but the nurturing, stable pair every child deserves. Lord Asriel treats her like an unfit soldier rather than a father's little princess. Mrs. Coulter pretends the part of maternal care, but only as a means of manipulation.

When we meet Will, he is caring for a mother who seems to have lost her mind. She can't possibly meet her son's needs for parental direction or provision, especially since Will's father is either dead or on an adventure he considers more important than paternal obligations. Though Will finally does meet him, their reunion is cut short when one of his father's former lovers kills him in vengeance, adding the separation of death to the pain of abandonment.

Even the gyptians, the most stable of family units, suffer the separation of kidnapping when Gobblers snatch children like Billy Costa away from the protection of home to experience the solitary nightmare of cutting.

In short, the children of Pullman's world (and his readers) never experience the grace, beauty, and security that flow from the interdependence and mutual submission that define a healthy home. Sending children off to boarding school or some other parentless context is a common British storytelling device. But unlike the Narnia tales or Harry Potter novels, Pullman's central characters exist in a world virtually devoid of stable, happy families. He has created a world of orphans.

Anyone who has spent time in or adopted someone from the foster-care system will tell you that the lives of orphans are indelibly marked by the experience. The clay of their hearts has been shaped in a harsh environment—making them less trusting, more aggressive, and fiercely independent. Who can blame them? Living with one foster parent after another or being passed over by one prospective parent after another sends a clear and hurtful message to the soul: "You don't belong."

Something similar occurs in children raised in abusive or troubled homes. They tend to be more defensive and on edge, unable to find their smiles.

Not surprisingly, then, the *His Dark Materials* trilogy exudes the aroma of an orphanage rather than a home. As a result, it takes itself far too seriously—as if someone drained any sense of humor from its pages. Granted, most traditional fairy stories deal with serious themes. But few maintain such a relentlessly portentous tone. Even Tolkien's *The Lord of the Rings* series, with its dark themes and oppressive villains, provides readers with moments of redemptive joy—from the charm of hobbit culture to the hilarious interventions of old Tom Bombadil. Not so with Pullman. His characters reflect the serious, distrustful tenor of children turned into solitary survivors. If invited to a holiday meal with other children, they would be the kids standing in the corner scoffing at the playful, trusting innocence displayed among those nurtured in maternal care and paternal stability.

Pullman describes Lyra as one raised in a masculine world of university Scholars, men who had "taught her, chastised her, consoled her, given her little presents," and "chased her away from the fruit trees in the garden." They were the closest thing she had to family. "They might even have felt like a family," Pullman says, "if she knew what a family was."[1]

Readers of *His Dark Materials* find themselves journeying through worlds filled with adults and children who, like Lyra, display little of the fruit typically nurtured in the soil of a happy home—such as laughter, peace, and the calm confidence of knowing you belong. With the possible exception of several gyptians, none of Pullman's characters have experienced what it means to live in a family led by a strong, loving father.

Anyone who attends a Christian church will likely hear about a God who is called "our Father which art in heaven." And while the minister might proclaim that reality of God until he is blue in the face, if those listening remember or live with an abusive, detached dad, the positive truth will be overshadowed by negative experience.

Describing what the Bible teaches us about God is like

reading the lines of a musical score. Living in a happy home, however, is akin to attending the symphony, where our spirits are immersed in the beauty and power of something one must hear to love. It is then that we understand the meaning of the notes and understand the composer's true gift. Lyra never heard that beautiful music, and as a result, she—and Pullman himself—reflects a warped view of the one others call "our heavenly Father."

It is always risky and unfair to speculate, but some have suggested that Pullman's admitted atheism and clear antagonism to Christianity could have been influenced by the experience of losing his own father at the vulnerable age of seven.

New York University professor of psychology Paul Vitz offers intriguing insight in his book *Faith of the Fatherless*. Vitz makes a case for atheism as one consequence of an unhealthy or absent relationship with dear old dad. "I am quite convinced that for every person strongly swayed by rational argument, there are countless others more affected by non-rational, psychological factors. . . . I propose, then, that irrational, often neurotic, psychological barriers to belief in God are of great importance." [2]

Vitz examines the actual childhood experience of some of history's most famous atheists, including Voltaire, Nietzsche, Freud, and Bertrand Russell. All of them had a poor relationship or no relationship with their fathers, a sharp contrast to the relatively healthy relationships found among those on the other end of faith's spectrum, such as Blaise Pascal, Søren Kierkegaard, and G. K. Chesterton.

He concludes that there is a psychological aspect to unbelief, particularly when expressed as the kind of characterizations of God encountered in Pullman's writings. Of course, this is not the whole story. After all, for every fatherless atheist who attacks Christianity, there are believers who find solace in the fatherhood of God despite an abusive or absent parent—C. S. Lewis and J. R. R. Tolkien are two obvious examples. Still, we cannot ignore the influence of painful experiences on one's belief system. For better or worse, what happens to us seems to trigger a strong response in us.

What happened to Lyra, Will, and the other children seems to have triggered a vitriolic reaction against the idea of God as loving Father who deserves our admiration, replacing Him with a weak, elderly tyrant who deserves to die. In the process, Pullman turns us all into orphans.

LIGHT
God is a loving Father, not a cruel tyrant.

WILL AND GRACE

Mrs. Cooper balanced her frail form on the edge of a Windsor chair and studied the odd pair occupying the sofa: the mother, distraught and childlike, her flyaway hair unkempt, her smile tentative and withdrawn; the son, fierce yet tender, his eyes full of anxious love, his jaw set with a determination that almost frightened the old woman. Hand in hand the two of them sat in the ruddy glow of the evening sunlight, each face a mirror image of the other except for the sharply contrasting expressions they bore. Mrs. Cooper could not remember when she had seen anything quite so unsettling.

She knew them, of course. Not that she had ever been well

acquainted with the woman. *She* was only a dim and shadowy figure in the old lady's memory. But the boy, Will Parry, had been a promising piano student—a child who stuck to business and spoke only when he had something important to say.

"She won't be any trouble," he was saying now. "She just needs someone to look after her for a few days. Someone kind and understanding." He showed Mrs. Cooper the clothing and food he'd brought for her.

Mrs. Cooper objected, suggesting he contact a doctor, a neighbor, maybe someone from social services. Yet Will wouldn't back down. He assured her his mother wasn't ill, just worried and confused. If not for some urgent business he had to attend to, he would be caring for her himself.

The old woman got up from her chair and stood looking down into his glittering steel-blue eyes. There was pain written there—pain and fear and loneliness—as well as grim resolution. Something in his face was so adamant, so decisive and intransigent, that the old woman had no choice except to yield. Suddenly overcome, she sat down heavily and passed a hand over her eyes. Reluctantly she agreed to keep Will's mother with her.

Will bent to kiss his mother and hugged her tightly. Then, without looking back, he walked straight to the front door, Mrs. Cooper following at his heels. Opening the door slowly, he peered cautiously and deliberately into the street. The sun had set, and the shadows between the houses were deepening. He turned once more to thank Mrs. Cooper. Then he was gone.

*　*　*　*　*

In the final pages of *The Amber Spyglass*, when the major conflicts and struggles of *His Dark Materials* have all been resolved and the epic story is drawing to its conclusion, Lyra, sitting at the foot of a white sand dune on a moonlit beach in another world, asks the rebel angel Xaphania why she can no longer read the alethiometer, a rare, compasslike object that Pullman has defined as "a device for the divination of truth."[1] The angel's answer is telling.

> "You read it by grace," she explains, "and you can regain it by work. . . . But your reading will be even better then, after a lifetime of thought and effort, because it will come from conscious understanding. Grace attained like that is deeper and fuller than grace that comes freely, and furthermore, once you've gained it, it will never leave you."[2]

Xaphania's statement won't sit well with Christians, who affirm the primacy of pure, unadulterated grace: God's free, unmerited favor toward all who trust in Him. But it accords perfectly with the outlook and behavior of one of the trilogy's two central figures: Lyra's traveling companion, fellow adventurer, and late-found romantic interest—Will Parry.

Will, as his name suggests, is a boy of fierce independence and strong determination. He's the image incarnate of what it means to survive by ingenuity, skill, and sheer "want-to." The circumstances of his life have left him with no alternative. His father went missing while he was still an infant. His mother's mental stability has been slipping ever since. He comes from a home where the natural parent-child relationship has been reversed—where it falls to *him* to see that his mother is fed and clothed, that she doesn't do anything to harm herself or attract unnecessary attention, and that she's protected from her own irrational anxieties and the cruel insensitivity of others. As a result, he's a firm believer in hard work and self-sufficiency.

Will can do things that the average twelve-year-old never even has to think about. He can cook and clean and manage money. He can run a household and do the laundry. He can whip up an omelette, wash the dishes, hitchhike to Oxford, confer with lawyers, and conduct independent research into his father's whereabouts. He can defend his mother against threats and enemies. He's even capable of killing if the situation calls for it.

Will, in short, has mastered the art of solitary self-reliance. He trusts no one but himself. He needs nobody else. The concluding lines of William Henley's famous poem "Invictus" could easily serve as his personal anthem and creed:

> *I am the master of my fate;*
> *I am the captain of my soul.*[3]

It's not surprising, then, that when the conversation on the moonlit beach turns to the subject of Will's future and the work he will undertake after returning to his own world, he responds to this particular challenge as he has responded to every other. "Whatever I do," he tells Xaphania decisively, "I will choose it, no one else."[4]

These aspects of Will's character are immediately apparent the very first time we meet him, in the opening scene of *The Subtle Knife*. From the moment he shows up on Mrs. Cooper's doorstep with his distracted mother in tow, we, like the perplexed old piano teacher herself, find ourselves marveling at the boy's unflinching obstinacy and the ease with which he asserts his will and assumes control of the situation. It's not that he's manipulative or pushy. It's just that he knows what has to be done, and he won't be deflected from doing it. After all, no one else is going to do it for him.

But there's an irony here—a subtle irony that Pullman himself can hardly have missed: Will demonstrates these traits of forcefulness and independence while in the very act of *asking for help*. For all his strength and courage and self-reliance, for all the suspicion with which he tends to regard other people, Will, at the very outset of his adventures, finds himself obliged to lean on someone else. He comes to Mrs. Cooper seeking grace. And grace—*free* grace—is exactly what he receives.

That's just the beginning, of course. As the story progresses, Pullman repeatedly reminds us that Will *feels* his need for grace acutely. He weeps when the burden of bearing the subtle knife is laid on his shoulders—and immediately receives unexpected and unorthodox comfort from Lyra's daemon, Pantalaimon.[5] He lies awake at night, worrying about his mother. He knows that she'd be safer with him; yet "he wanted her to look after him, too, as she'd done when he was very small."[6] He feels forlorn, like a little boy, and longs for his father "as a lost child yearns for home."[7]

Nor is Will the only character in the world of *His Dark Materials* who wrestles with this internal conflict between proud self-reliance and a desire to be upheld and sustained by someone else. Mary Malone, the former nun turned physicist, is of a similar mind. Like Will, Mary is a confirmed loner. She enjoys the challenge of life lived as a solo effort. She once loved an attractive Italian man, it's true, but not enough to form a permanent attachment. Later on, she actually lived with a man for a while but stopped short of committing herself to a long-term relationship. "So I'm on my own," she tells Will and Lyra during an extended afternoon session of baring her soul. "I'm solitary but happy, if you see what I mean."[8]

But somehow we *don't* quite see what she means. Somehow

we are left with a sense that Mary, for all her competence and self-assurance, is uncertain and ill at ease. Somehow we get the feeling that Mary, like Will, desperately needs a touch of grace.

This impression is especially strong in her case, because her struggle is played out on a much higher level than Will's. It's not just the love, comfort, and assistance of other people that she resists. Mary has declared her independence from God Himself. She has rejected the Church, her childhood faith, and all the lofty spiritual values that once made her life worthwhile. She's "on her own" in the most profound and frightening sense of the phrase—a sensitive, personable, and intensely human young woman alone in a vast and luminous but coldly impersonal universe.

For Mary, then, there can be no free ride. If her existence is to have significance, she must achieve it by "work, effort, and conscious understanding." But she doesn't find this easy. She, too, knows how it feels to be "a lost child yearning for home." When Will asks her whether she "misses God," she answers without hesitation.

> "Yes, terribly. . . . And what I miss most is the sense of being connected to the whole of the universe. I used to feel I was connected to God like that, and because he was there, I was connected to the whole of his creation. But if he's not there, then . . ."[9]

It's true that Pullman, in the very next chapter, shows Mary overcoming this feeling of disconnectedness by realizing that the universe can only be saved by reversing the leakage of Dust—that the wind, moon, clouds, leaves, and grass are "trying to hold back the Dust flood" and that *she* has a part to play in helping them achieve their aim. It's a stirring passage. But the wording the author uses to express his ideas begs a fundamental question about the true nature of the thing Mary is seeking: "Matter *loved* Dust. It didn't want to see it go."[10] This is the meaning and purpose of everything.

In resorting to the language of love, Pullman has in effect brought us back to the issue of grace. For love, as anyone knows who has really experienced it, cannot be gained by work or won by merit. Love is its own justification. Love lifts us up when we cannot lift ourselves. Love, as the hymn declares, is "lord of heaven and earth";[11] and God, as the Scripture insists, *is* love Himself (1 John 4:16). Dust and elementary particles cannot love. People can. Once again our attention is directed to the wonder of a universe centered upon the deep mystery of *relationship*—the miracle of the eternal *I and Thou*.

It's a matter of the utmost significance that at the end of *His Dark Materials* these two stubbornly independent and self-reliant characters, Will Parry and Mary Malone, wind up together in just such a relationship of mutual affection and interdependence. Upon re-entering their own world—*our* world—at the close of their incredible journey, they find, against all expectation, that they *need* one another.

"We're both on our own," says Mary. "And we're both in trouble. . . . If you'll let me, I'll be your friend for the rest of our lives." For Will, these words were like thunder out of a clear blue sky.

> Mary was a friend. He had a friend. It was true. He'd never thought of that.[12]

We all need that kind of friend: a friend whose love, loyalty, and faithfulness cannot be earned but are simply lavished upon us without warning or explanation. A friend who relates to us not on the basis of what we can achieve by our own determination and hard work, but simply on the basis of pure, untrammeled *grace*.

How good it is to know that such a Friend exists and that, as the Bible puts it, He "sticks closer than a brother" (Proverbs 18:24). He has proven His friendship by laying down His life for us (John 15:13-14), and He has promised never to leave us or forsake us, "even to the end of the age" (Matthew 28:20).

There is no higher love, no greater grace than this.

LIGHT

Even the strongest among us desperately needs free grace.

"Angels?" said Serafina. "You mentioned them before. They are new to us. Can you explain them?"

—*The Subtle Knife*, CHAPTER 6, "LIGHTED FLIERS"

ANGELS

The two witches, Serafina Pekkala and Ruta Skadi, listened intensely as Joachim Lorenz explained the horrific sight they had just witnessed. Like vampires drinking blood, spectral forms had sucked the life essence from nearly every adult in Joachim's traveling party—leaving the distraught and now orphaned children untouched.

These terrorizing beings, Joachim explained, seemed to have invaded his world through windows between the worlds left open by careless philosophers and explorers. He and the woman in his traveling party had fled at the sight of the Specters, not because they were cowards, but because they knew they were defenseless against them. Some must preserve themselves in order to care for the children once these ghostly creatures had had their fill. He and the woman had returned to gather and guide the weeping little ones.

After sharing everything he knew of the specters, Joachim asked Serafina and Ruta why they had come to his world. They were looking for a child, Lyra Belacqua, they told him, before asking if he had seen such a girl traveling alone.

"No, but we saw angels headed for the Pole."

Yet another mystery to Serafina Pekkala. "What are angels?" she wondered aloud.

Joachim described marveling at the sight of vast, shining troops of angels, armed for battle. His grandfather had spoken of a time when such sights were more common, angels passing through this world. But for him, it was something new—possibly the sign of a vast heavenly conflict on the horizon.

"Angels are new to us. Can you tell us more about them?" Serefina's curiosity unleashed a series of fascinating details:

These spirit beings were without bodies, or at least had bodies quite different from those of humans.

They called themselves *bene elim*. Others called them Watchers.

Winged creatures, they shone like fireflies in the sky as they passed through this world on their way to others. They were said to be carrying messages from heaven.

Joachim also mentioned rumors that, in ancient days, the

angels came to his world and bred with the people. Serafina didn't find this so surprising, since she herself had fallen in love with men.

Suddenly, as he peered into the vast evening sky, Joachim called to his companions and pointed upward to what he knew to be a troop of passing angels. Ruta Skadi stood to make her leave, intent on finding out where they were headed.

Racing toward the angels, Ruta could gradually make out their forms. Sunlight seemed to shine upon them despite the darkness. Like winged, naked humans with deeply muscled frames, they were taller than men and unarmed—they did not appear hostile. She noticed that three of the beings were male; two female.

As she cried out to them, they turned in unison to face her, their piercing glares more penetrating and unmoved than those of any humans she had ever encountered. Though they told her little, Ruta was sure of their mission.

She chose to join them as they traveled through this and other worlds toward the assembly of soldiers in Asriel's charge. And despite being more than four hundred years old, she seemed a mere child in their presence.

* * * * *

As children most of us believed in angels, those mighty guardians watching over our slumber. We figured we never saw them because, like Santa Claus and the Tooth Fairy, they appeared in the dark when we were asleep, and most importantly, because they were transparent. Still, we believed. After all, Mom and Dad and our Sunday school teacher told us they existed.

Of course, we did get an idea of what they looked like while flipping through the pictures in the thick family Bible, or touring the religious-art section of the Christian bookstore, or passing the icons hanging on our church walls. Sometimes they were beautiful women with flowing gowns and gentle wings of pure white. Other times they seemed powerful—armor-clad men with expansive, forceful wings twice the size of their massive frames. And occasionally they appeared as small children with tiny wings—like Cupid without his bow. With the exception of the endearing Irish chap named Clarence who helped save George Bailey in *It's a Wonderful Life*, angels always had wings.

Other than a vague notion of unseen guardian angels or heavenly warriors or even retired human beings playing harps, however, few of us have developed a solid conception of these mysterious beings. So when they show up in Philip Pullman's trilogy, it is difficult to decipher how much or how little his characters reflect Christian theology—especially when reading that angels once bred with men and women. How closely do Pullman's angels mirror those found in the Bible and Frank Capra films?

Even a cursory reading of Pullman's novels suggests that

the author, like the rest of us, had a childhood belief in angels influenced by church tradition. But as with the Tooth Fairy, he seems to have abandoned that belief by adulthood. Still, a residue of Christian theology remains. Several specific examples suggest this.

Joachim Lorenz, the Specter-fleeing character in *The Subtle Knife*, described angels as ones who carry messages from heaven. "That's their calling," he explained. From a biblical perspective, angels are indeed messengers of God. They traveled to Abraham to tell him of God's promise to give Sarah a child. They went into Sodom to call Lot out of his wicked hometown. They told Mary that she would give birth to God's Son and proclaimed the arrival of Messiah to shepherds abiding in the fields. And, of course, angels had the privilege of telling the women at the tomb of Jesus' resurrection from the dead.

The witch, Ruta Skadi, accurately observed that each angel "was distinctly an individual." Christian tradition tells us they are spiritual creatures with intelligence and free will, not some mindless assembly of passive beings. In fact, angels have names. Gabriel, for example, had the honored role of announcing the pending births of both John the Baptist and Jesus Himself. So Pullman's description of spirit beings with individual identities reflects a biblical perspective.

Another similarity is angelic intervention in human affairs. Baruch and Balthamos, for example, are angels who alert and protect Will. Despite their lack of bodily form, angels do indeed have the power to assist and affect men and women, as seen in several scriptural passages. Angels led Hagar and her son, Ishmael, to water, preserving what would become the Arab race. An angel stayed the hand of Abraham just before he lowered a knife to Isaac's throat and stopped a donkey dead in its tracks to get stubborn Balaam's attention. An army of angels amassed on the hillside just before battle, shoring up the wavering confidence of Elisha's sidekick when he finally saw "the hills full of horses and chariots of fire all around."[1] They even came down and ministered to Jesus after His season of temptation in the wilderness.

But what of the bizarre notion of angels engaging in sexual relations with human beings? Pullman clearly departs from Christian tradition with that idea. Or does he? Strange as it seems, he is not the first to suggest the possibility. It comes from certain interpretations of an obscure reference in the book of Genesis.

When men began to increase in number on the earth and daughters were born to them, the sons of God saw that the daughters of men were beautiful, and they married any of them they chose. Then the LORD said, "My spirit will not contend with man forever, for he is mortal; his days will be a hundred and twenty years." The Nephilim were on the earth in those days—and also afterward—when the sons of God went to the daughters of men and had children by them. They were the heroes of old, men of renown. (GENESIS 6:1-4, NIV)

Bible scholars and commentators have wrestled with this passage for generations. What could it mean? Since the passage gives enough information to feed speculation but too little to provide clarity, opinions abound. Some think the "sons of God" were the line of Seth, Adam's righteous son, while the "daughters of men" were the wicked Cainites. This theory says the passage is merely a description of how widespread wickedness had become at this time.

A second possibility is that these were indeed angels engaging in sexual relations with women. But the angels of Pullman's world, like true angels, have no bodies. So how could this be?

A third explanation, one Pullman's imagination seems to have borrowed, says that the Genesis passage suggests demonic forces overtook human bodies in order to enjoy the ravenous delights of physical intimacy otherwise beyond the experience of spirit beings. The most explicit indication that this might be Pullman's view occurs in *The Amber Spyglass* during a conversation between Mrs. Coulter and Metatron, a villainous angelic being.

> "When I was a man," he said, "I had wives in plenty, but none was as lovely as you."
>
> "When you were a man?"
>
> "When I was a man, I was known as Enoch, the son of Jared, the son of Mahalalel, the son of Kenan, the

son of Enosh, the son of Seth, the son of Adam. I lived
on earth for sixty-five years, and then the Authority
took me to his Kingdom."[2]

Astute readers may recognize the line of Enoch who,
in Pullman's world, was taken up to the Kingdom of "the
Authority" without dying. In Genesis chapter five we learn of
the real Enoch who descended from Jared, Mahalalel, Kenan,
Enosh, Seth, and Adam. The real Enoch, like Pullman's copy,
was "taken away" by God.

"And you had many wives," Mrs. Coulter inquired.

"I loved their flesh. And I understood it when the sons of
Heaven fell in love with the daughters of earth, and I pleaded
their cause with the Authority. But his heart was fixed against
them."[3]

The angel Metatron, then, is portrayed to be one of those
"sons of God" who was intimate with the "daughters of
men." Later, he earned a promotion to angelic status. Despite
such an impressive promotion, however, Metatron remains a
created being like those described in the Bible.

The big difference between scriptural angels and Pullman's
is that his spontaneously formed from the Dust generated
when matter became conscious of itself. Pullman's "good"
angels are actually rebels opposing the tyrannical rule of a
power-hungry, malevolent Authority, whereas in the biblical

universe, good angels worship and serve a holy, loving God who created them.

So despite the many similarities and Pullman's Bible-based speculations, the fundamental nature of angels in his world differs dramatically from that of Christian tradition. Angels are not promoted human beings or creatures spun from Dust but distinct creations of God with a specific purpose.

They, like us, were made to serve their Creator and worship Him forever.

> *Bless the LORD, you His angels,*
> *Who excel in strength, who do His word,*
> *Heeding the voice of His word.*
> *Bless the LORD, all you His hosts,*
> *You ministers of His, who do His pleasure.*
> *Bless the LORD, all His works,*
> *In all places of His dominion.*
> *Bless the LORD, O my soul!*
>
> (PSALM 103:20-22)

LIGHT

Angels proclaim the glory of God
and the salvation of men.

> *"And what is the Authority?
> Is he God?"*
>
> —*The Amber Spyglass*, CHAPTER 2,
> "BALTHAMOS AND BARUCH"

THE AUTHORITY

As he pulled the breach closed behind them, Will felt the impact of the spear he had narrowly escaped. Now safely beyond its piercing power, hands still trembling from the sudden peril requiring quick thinking and even quicker action, he breathed a sigh of relief while glancing at his barely visible companions. Balthamos and Baruch were trying to regain their own strained composure.

Moments earlier Will had been sitting around an evening campfire calmly discussing options with his new friends. They urgently wanted to take him to Lord Asriel. But despite his father's charge that Will bring the knife to the great commander, he insisted on keeping the powerful tool until he found Lyra.

Having access to flying angels, Will took advantage of the situation to learn as much as possible about her location. It was then, right after Baruch informed him that she was safe and nearby, that a look of panic overtook Balthamos's mostly transparent face. He looked like a soldier reacting to an enemy bullet. After ordering Will to douse the fire, he quietly told him that the enemy had found them.

Suddenly an immense power propelled itself downward and crashed into Balthamos. Baruch leapt into the fray, and the two angels were engaged in mortal combat with a third angelic being. Even though the intruder seemed much stronger than either of them, they managed to wrestle him to the ground before calling to Will.

"Use the knife; cut a way out!" They needed an opening into another world. Any world, as long as it got them away from the danger of which this sole attacker was merely a part.

Just then Will managed to glance upward to see clouds swirling into an ominous funnel of destructive intentions. Something else, something much deadlier, would soon join the invasion. Balthamos noticed as well and again ordered Will to cut an opening into another world. At that same moment, a second invader raised a spear, aiming at Will's unprotected torso.

And then—the humid air of a sandy beach beneath a luminous moon. All three safe from a world of impending doom vanishing behind, like children caught in a sudden downpour who escape to the protective cover of a zipped tent. Only instead of a cramped nylon dome, their zipper opened an entire world filled with fern trees and a long, sandy shore.

Balthamos told Will they'd just fought Metatron, the Authority's most powerful Regent. Will had heard of the Authority before. From what he had pieced together, it seemed like another name for what they called God in his world.

Over the next several minutes, Balthamos told the whole tale; that the Authority—also called God, the Creator, the Lord, Yahweh, El, Adonai, the King, the Father, the Almighty—had taken those names for himself. In actuality, the Authority was nothing more than self-aware matter. Dust that had formed itself into a living being. As the first to spring forth from the particles, the Authority lied to all who came after, telling them he was their creator and deserved their allegiance. He had never been the creator, but a mere angel like Baruch and Balthamos. The first and most powerful angel, yes. But not a creator.

Eventually one wiser than the Authority arose, Balthamos told Will. After finding out the truth, she was banished. Now he and Baruch served this great angel, Xaphania.

Suddenly, the conflict into which Will had fallen took form. These angels, as well as Lord Asriel, Lyra, and his now-dead father, were all part of a great rebellion against a deceptive tyrant; one who pretended to be more than he was, an oppressor who should be overthrown to free living beings to rule their own lives rather than submit to his illegitimate reign.

With the knife safe from the Authority's thieving regent, Will became more determined than ever to find Lyra before handing it over to Lord Asriel. No matter how important this campaign to overthrow the Tyrant, the knife allowed Will to escape from the likes of Metatron when needed. And he had an unsettling feeling that this was not the last time such power would prove useful.

* * * * *

"The current insanity of heaven," argues Lucifer in Mark Rutland's *Behind the Glittering Mask*, "is manifestly obvious in the Tyrant's wicked determination to be recognized as GOD— the God, exclusively God. What monstrous ego! The Tyrant wants one universe with himself as its only God, directing all wills by his will."[1] So goes one of the fallen angel's challenges to his rival, the archangel Michael, in this fictitious account.

Defiant as it may be, the devil's speech does appeal to our sense of fairness and autonomy. Why does God demand our worship? Is He such an egomaniac that He requires constant praise and adoration to feel good about Himself? Why does He require our submission to His will rather than our own?

We know we shouldn't ask such questions. But we can't

help ourselves. We bristle at a God who seems self-serving, domineering, and proud. And we long to claim our "rightful" place as master of our own destinies, lord of our own lives.

And that is precisely why so many of us resonate with those in Pullman's trilogy who risk everything to join a second war in heaven. A war that seeks to put "the Authority" in his rightful place—the grave.

When asked Lord Asriel's intentions, one of his servants explains that "he's gone a-searching for the dwelling place of the Authority Himself, and he's a-going to destroy Him."[2]

When Ruta Skadi returned from her encounter with Lord Asriel, she explained to her sister witches that the commander invited them "to join his army against the Authority." She told them that he had opened her eyes to cruelties and horrors committed in the name of the Authority, cruelties designed to destroy the "joys and the truthfulness of life." She celebrates the daring of one willing to "make war on the Creator!"[3]

When Mrs. Coulter asked the great angel Xaphania whether she had been part of the heavenly rebellion in ages past, she replied, "Yes. And since then I have been wandering between many worlds. Now I have pledged my allegiance to Lord Asriel, because I see in his great enterprise the best hope of destroying the tyranny at last."[4]

And the most offensive attack against the Authority comes from a reformed Mrs. Coulter who finally shakes off the teachings of her church.

"Well, where is God," said Mrs. Coulter, "if he's alive? And why doesn't he speak anymore? . . . Is he still alive, at some inconceivable age, decrepit and demented, unable to think or act or speak and unable to die, a rotten hulk? And if that is his condition, wouldn't it be the most merciful thing, the truest proof of our love for God, to seek him out and give him the gift of death?"[5]

If this Authority is anything like Balthamos and Baruch describe him to Will, we might be inclined to agree with Mrs. Coulter. After all, who needs an illegitimate, power-hungry ruler who gained his power through deception? Why shouldn't we join forces to overthrow such a deity?

Before enlisting, however, let's return to Mark Rutland's depiction of a debate between Lucifer and Michael over pride. Specifically, Lucifer accuses God of possessing a monstrous ego, claiming himself to be the liberator of an oppressed humanity.

"I do not want others to do my will," Lucifer argues. "I want them to do their own. I alone desire that all will their own wills. The Tyrant is obsessed with convincing men and angels that he alone is God. I am not offended that the Tyrant calls himself a god. By all means, let him be a god. For that matter, I am willing for everything breathing to be a god. Let us all be gods! Had it not been for me, Adam would never have known his destiny as a god."[6]

Same song, seven-billionth verse. Why should we remain under God's oppressive thumb? Why can't we break free and discover our true selves—and the joy of individual autonomy with no overarching authority telling us what to do? In the spirit of John Lennon, let's imagine a world with no heaven, no countries, no authority! In the words of the serpent, let's take and eat the fruit of rebellion so that our eyes will be opened and we can "be like God."

And what if God did not make us after all? What if we simply came to be of our own power—self-aware matter turned self-confident beings? That is precisely what Pullman suggests happened to every living being—including the Authority himself. In the words of Balthamos:

"He was never the creator. He was an angel like ourselves—the first angel, true, the most powerful, but he was formed of Dust as we are, and Dust is only a name for what happens when matter begins to understand itself."[7]

The God of *His Dark Materials* bears little resemblance to the God of Christianity as revealed in Jesus Christ, one who "being in very nature God, did not consider equality with God something to be grasped, but made himself nothing, taking the very nature of a servant" (Philippians 2:6-7, NIV). He was not an egomaniac, but one who described himself as meek, lowly, and humble of heart (see Matthew 11:29, NIV).

The God of Pullman's trilogy instead bears striking resemblance to another biblical character—the first angel who deceived others so that they would submit to his illicit authority. In other words, "a liar and the father of lies" (John 8:44, NIV).

Not surprisingly, Balthamos's description of the Authority's beginning finds inspiration in *Paradise Lost*, where Milton's Lucifer describes his own inception:

> *Th'Apostate, and more haughty thus repli'd*
> *'That we were form'd then say'st thou? and the work*
> *Of secondary hands, by task transferr'd*
> *From Father to his Son? strange point and new!*
> *Doctrine which we would know whence learnt: who saw*
> *When this creation was? remember'st thou*
> *Thy making, while the Maker gave thee being?*
> *We know no time when we were not as now;*
> *Know none before us, self-begot, self-rais'd*
> *By our own quick'ning power. . .*[8]

In arrogant refusal to acknowledge his true origin, Lucifer manages to deceive even himself into believing he spawned his own creation: "self-begot, self raised, by our own quick'ning power."

The concept rings familiar to those of us living in a world that has abandoned the authority of a Creator. The idea of undirected evolutionary progress has become so popular because, in the spirit of Milton's rebel protagonist, it allows us to become our own gods. It provides an alibi for us to shed ourselves of God, so that we can delude ourselves into believing our own quickening power raised us out of the primordial mud. Or rather, out of the elementary particles Pullman calls Dust.

In the end, the Authority Lord Asriel's army hopes to overthrow—the God for whom Mrs. Coulter prescribes a merciful killing, the Tyrant angels hope to defeat—turns out to be a familiar enemy. Despite the names Pullman attaches, the Authority is really none other than Lucifer—that one who carries the foul odor of rebellion against the sanity of submission.

"Why must there be only one god?" asks Rutland's debating Lucifer.

"That is simply the way it is," comes Michael's reply. "There are billions of rabbits who know themselves to be rabbits. There are billions of mice and mules and men. And there are legions of angels. As long as they know themselves to be mice or men or angels, all is well. But when they think themselves to be gods, the madness of your rebellion eats out their insides."[9]

*Hear, O Israel: The L*ORD *our God, the L*ORD *is one!*
(DEUTERONOMY 6:4)

One feels solidarity with Asriel's campaign to dethrone an illicit god who deceived, coerced, and intimidated his way to the top. A "deity" who is not creator but creature—not Lord but liar.

LIGHT

Lucifer, not God, is the true Tyrant.

MAGISTERIUM

A naphtha lamp hissed in a sconce beside the door, sending a spray of soft yellow light rippling up the bare plaster walls and across the low-beamed ceiling. A red candle flickered at the edge of a rough wooden table, flinging erratic shadows over the dark spines of the leather-bound volumes in the bookcases. Through the open window came the muffled sounds of the streets of Geneva; while within the small and sparsely furnished chamber, more like a monk's cell than the study of a powerful Church magistrate, the hushed air was electric with subdued anticipation. Father MacPhail, president of the Church's Consistorial Court of Discipline, lifted his head from prayer.

Laying his powerful, long-fingered hands on the dark head of the priest who sat opposite him, Father MacPhail promised the younger man preemptive absolution for the actions he was about to take in the service of Holy Church.

The young man gazed up at the court's president with blazing eyes. He whispered his thanks before taking the older priest's hand in his own and earnestly kissing the gold signet ring. He was intent on doing whatever was necessary to destroy Dust and the hideous burden of sin—even though it meant murdering Lyra.

President MacPhail smiled, his heart warming towards his earnest young apprentice. They rose and stood facing one another in the dancing candlelight. Reaching across the table, he opened a cabinet drawer and pulled out a thick sheaf of papers. As he handed them to the other priest, he explained that the documents contained everything they'd been able to discover about the woman—whom he called the Tempter—and the girl, Lyra.

"Study these papers carefully, my dear Luis. Remember you go with my blessing," he said.

Never before had the president addressed him by his first name. The priest felt tears of joy sting his eyes as he kissed Father MacPhail good-bye.

SHEDDING LIGHT
on His Dark Materials

* * * * *

What is the Church?

This is one of the major questions raised by the action of *His Dark Materials*. And the answers that author Philip Pullman proposes in the process of crafting his epic tale are anything but flattering. For as the drama unfolds and the plot thickens, it is the Church that emerges as the story's undisputed villain—the agency of evil *par excellence*. [1]

In the second chapter of *The Subtle Knife*, during a speech that follows a scene of ecclesiastically authorized torture, Queen Ruta Skadi warns her fellow witches that war is in the making. "I don't know who will join with us," she says, "but I know whom we must fight."

> It is the Magisterium, the Church. For all its history . . .
> it's tried to suppress and control every natural impulse.
> And when it can't control them, it cuts them out. . . .
> That is what the Church does, and every church is the
> same: control, destroy, obliterate every good feeling.
> So if a war comes, and the Church is on one side of it,
> we must be on the other.[2]

Ruta Skadi is not the only one who feels this way. Her perspective is shared by nearly all of Pullman's most inspirational and sympathetic characters. The fatherly John Faa, for instance, is uneasy about the growing power of the Church, which, in his view, has been "getting more commanding" in recent times.[3] The heroic Lord Asriel "has never found himself at ease with the doctrines of the Church," notes Thorold, Asriel's longtime servant, and so he has decided to oppose it and destroy its tyrannical God.[4] The brave and wise shaman, John Parry, is determined to help Asriel in any way he can "because the task he's undertaken is the greatest in human history."[5] The venerable angel Xaphania agrees. As for Mary Malone, she's long since thrown off the yoke of religious devotion, having discovered that Christianity is just "a very powerful and convincing mistake."[6] Everyone, it seems, is keen as mustard to get out from under the thumb of the Church.

And not without good reason. For as we've already seen, it's *the Church* that divides human beings from their own souls. It's *the Church* that kidnaps little children and ships them off to die in a concentration camp. It's *the Church* that exercises Naziesque control over the lives of individuals, squelches joy, promotes brutality, and goes to unthinkable lengths in its efforts to impose its ironclad will upon society. It's *the Church* that sets itself up as the unrivaled perpetrator of man's inhumanity to man. "We have a thousand years of experience in this Church of ours," says Mrs. Coulter as she ruthlessly breaks the fingers of a captive witch. "We can draw out your suffering endlessly."[7]

Why does the Church of *His Dark Materials* do such horrendous things? The answer is simple: It behaves this way because of *what it is*. And what it *is* is masterfully captured for us in the brief episode renarrated above.[8] Here, in a few deft and deadly strokes, Pullman paints a chillingly accurate and intimate portrait of an organization that exists solely to preserve its own interests and advance its own organizational aims—an institution so big, so influential, and so self-absorbed that its own sustenance has become the primary reason for its being.

Like most tyrannical establishments, this Church isn't necessarily interested in cruelty for cruelty's sake. On the contrary, it oppresses and kills because it *has* to. Its survival depends upon its capacity to control. At the heart of its "tangle of courts, colleges, and councils"[9] lies an all-consuming obsession with power—not power as an end in itself, but power as a means to achieving supposedly good and righteous objectives. Could there be a more fitting name for the ruling hierarchy of this organization than the one Pullman gives it? *Magisterium* is a Latin title that has links with the English word *mastery*.[10]

This picture of the Church stands in direct contrast to the one we find in the New Testament. For as any careful student of Scripture knows, the biblical Church isn't an *organization* at all. It's an *organism*: the living, breathing Body of the Savior, Jesus Christ, who is Himself the Church's living head (Colossians 1:18). It's the continuing physical presence on earth of the Crucified and Risen Lord—the hands and feet of the Suffering Servant who "bore our griefs and carried our sorrows" and who, as a result, was "despised and rejected of men" (Isaiah 53:3-4, KJV).

It's worth mentioning here that Jesus is oddly missing from the pages of *His Dark Materials*. His name is mentioned only twice—both times by Mary Malone, the former nun turned scientist—and in neither case do we get the impression that His life, His words, His works, and His character are in any way central to the trilogy's vision of the Church. Apparently Pullman realizes that the villainy of the Magisterium, an essential ingredient of the tale, would be severely compromised were he to connect it in any way with the figure of Christ.

Meanwhile, those of us who know the Bible recognize that there can be no Church without Jesus. What's more, we understand that as the Body of Christ, the New Testament Church has no institutional agenda. Like its founder, it possesses no earthly status and wields no worldly power. It does not need to dominate society or destroy its enemies. Rather than a gang of oppressors, it is a community of the oppressed: the scum of the earth, the "offscouring of all things" (1 Corinthians 4:13), a collection of the "destitute, afflicted, tormented" (Hebrews 11:37) who have found refuge in Jesus, the one and only Rock of their salvation. It exists solely to manifest the life, death, and sacrificial love of its Master. Its mission statement is summed up in the memorable words of the apostle Paul: "We do not preach ourselves, but Christ Jesus the Lord, and ourselves your bondservants for Jesus' sake" (2 Corinthians 4:5).

It's important to remember, of course, that the Church of *His Dark Materials* is mere fiction—a hypothetical entity in a dreamed-up parallel dimension. In some ways it isn't really a church at all. As critic Andrew Leet observes, it's "a church in name only, an empty shell run by 'ancient and rheumy-eyed' men who are superstitious of, and hostile toward, everything outside their sphere of control."[11] Those of us who identify with the New Testament model of the Church and consider ourselves faithful members of the *true* Body of Christ are free to disregard this disturbing figment of Philip Pullman's literary imagination.

Or are we?

Obviously not. For the truth of the matter, as anyone must realize who has eyes to see and a heart to understand, is quite the opposite. If we take an honest look at history and current events, we'll have to admit that *power*—the desire to seize it and use it, even for good and beneficial purposes—has frequently led the Church of our own world to betray its birthright and abandon its rightful calling. Here, as in Lyra's universe, the quest for control has all too often turned otherwise good and well-meaning people into heartless tyrants. As Pullman himself observes, it has provided them with an irresistible incentive to convert their belief in God into "the most wonderful excuse for behaving badly."[12] That's because power, once gained, has to be retained. A position once occupied has to be defended. Organizational structures, once put in place, have to be maintained. And that means doing whatever it takes to stay on top of the pile—a mode of operation that is extremely difficult to reconcile with the cross and the crown of thorns.

Jesus understood this. That's why, when the multitudes came to take Him by force and make Him king, He slipped away and hid Himself on the mountain (John 6:15). That's why, when the devil offered Him a chance at world dominion, He refused in no uncertain terms (Matthew 4:8-10). That's why, when Pilate prodded Him with questions about the nature and meaning of His messianic mission, He returned such a strange and enigmatic reply: "My kingdom is not of this world. If My kingdom were of this world, My servants would fight, so that I should not be delivered to the Jews; but now My kingdom is not from here" (John 18:36).

This, then, is what the Church of Jesus really is: not an agency of authoritarian control, but an outpost of that *other Kingdom*—the Kingdom that stands above the fray of the never-ending scuffle for temporal power. And just as in the case of Pullman's Church, what this Church *is* should determine how it *behaves*; for "it is enough for a disciple that he be like his teacher, and a servant like his master" (Matthew 10:25).

LIGHT

The Church is not called to power, but to suffering and service.

> *"It would be a close fight, but Lord Asriel would win, because he is passionate and daring and he believes his cause is just."*
>
> —*The Subtle Knife*, CHAPTER 13, "ÆSAHAETTR"

REBEL TO THE WRONG

Standing atop the adamant tower, a monolith of sheer basalt looming high above the mountain peak like a fist upraised against the sky, Lord Asriel leaned upon the battlements and fitted his eye to the telescope. He squinted as he swung the lens westward, then grunted with satisfaction as the object he sought swept suddenly into view—a small white blur, just barely discernible against the hazy glare above the horizon, which grew in magnitude and clarity as he focused the instrument and pressed the eyepiece firmly against his brow.

At last, he turned to his chief of staff, the African king Ogunwe. He invited him to look at the distant object too.

The king stooped to peer through the glass. He and Lord Asriel were now sure that the Authority and his allies were bringing the battle to them. They were witnessing the approach of the Clouded Mountain, the flying citadel of the Authority. They were under siege.

Moments later a smudge of darker gray had emerged from the spot of cloud and was surging and billowing around it like smoke from a chimney. Asriel raised an eyebrow. King Ogunwe lifted his field glasses for a better look.

Hordes of angels, the army he and Lord Asriel would be facing, were spreading out like smoke throughout the sky. The men watched as the shroud of cloud gave way for just a moment, allowing them to glimpse guns and armaments. King Ogunwe lowered the glasses and made a sound of despair.

Suddenly fierce, Asriel seized the king's arm with a strong grip and stood facing him chin to chin. "Do you really believe that what *they* have can match what *we* have—this solid flesh and the passion that lives within it?" Though humans might be outnumbered, though they lived shorter lives and had weaker eyesight than the angels, Asriel insisted that he and his allies were physically stronger and would prevail.

Relaxing his grip, Lord Asriel looked away toward the gathering shadow on the horizon. He and the king talked a few more minutes before King Ogunwe bowed and left the room.

But Lord Asriel, clenching his fists, turned once more toward the Clouded Mountain.

*   *   *   *   *

Robin Hood—not Errol Flynn, not Kevin Costner, but the *real* Robin Hood, the yeoman in Lincoln green who inhabits the haunting lines of the old English ballads and breathes through the lilting cadences of Howard Pyle's antique prose—is a cultural icon we can't afford to lose in this age of moral confusion and spiritual doubt. Robin is a symbol of righteous resistance, a clear image of what it means to go against the flow in a world gone awry.

Technically speaking, Robin Hood is an outlaw: a desperado, a renegade, a dangerous public enemy. He flouts established rules and regulations. He has little respect for magistrates and authorities. He steals from the rich, gives to the poor, and never passes up an opportunity to make the Sheriff of Nottingham look like a fool.

But Robin doesn't do these things out of malice. His actions are not those of a mere malcontent or troublemaker. Unlike James Dean, he isn't just a rebel without a cause. On the contrary, there's a definite method to the madness of his outlawry. At the deepest level, his deeds of poaching and thievery are expressions of loyalty to his rightful sovereign. He clings to the memory of King Richard the Lion-Hearted and fiercely opposes the rule of the wicked usurper John. He's not so much a criminal as a political dissident, an insurgent against the tyranny of an unjust regime. He's what singer-songwriter Dennis Agajanian calls a *rebel to the wrong*.[1]

Robin Hood's position is a great deal like that of Lord Asriel, Lyra Belacqua's father and one of the chief protagonists of *His Dark Materials*. Asriel, too, is an insurrectionist. He's "aiming a rebellion against the highest power of all. He's gone a-searching for the dwelling place of the Authority Himself, and he's a-going to destroy Him."[2] But he hasn't embarked upon this path of lawlessness out of pure meanness or because he has a chip on his shoulder. He's neither an idle rabble-rouser nor an ambitious power seeker. Instead, he's genuinely outraged at the abuses of a corrupt and all-powerful Church, perpetrated under the auspices of a false and cruel deity. "He showed me that to rebel was right and just," said Ruta Skadi, "when you considered what the agents of the Authority did in His name."[3] Like Robin Hood, Asriel is a rebel to the wrong.

There's been a fair amount of speculation about the significance of Asriel's name among literary critics. "'Asriel,'" says Burton Hatlen, "seems, to my ear, phonetically identical with 'Azrael,' the angel of death in many mythological traditions."[4] Lance Parkin and Mark Jones agree, though they point out that this same Azrael also appears as "an angel under the command of God" in the apocryphal book of Tobit. "Peculiarly," they add, apparently puzzled by this piece of information, "the modern first name *Azriel* means 'God helps' in Hebrew."[5] No wonder they're confused: Lord Asriel is the *last* person in the world who wants any kind of help from God.

But there *is* another possibility. *Asriel,* if formed from the Hebrew root *'sr,'*[6] "to restrict or imprison," could mean "God binds me"; this interpretation yields a word picture strikingly consonant with the description of Lyra's father given in the first chapter of *The Golden Compass*:

> All his movements were large and perfectly balanced, like those of a wild animal, and when he appeared in a room like this, he seemed a wild animal held in a cage too small for it.[7]

"A wild animal held in a cage too small for it." This is a perfect summation of Asriel's character. For unlike the juvenile delinquent whose only aim is to prove his manhood or "beat the system," Asriel doesn't rebel simply for the sake of rebelling. He's more like a lion, or like his daemon, Stelmaria, the snow leopard: a beast born free, snatched from its home on the heath, and thrust into the cruel confinement of a city zoo. He feels intensely the injustice of his captivity; the very laws of nature demand that he burst his bonds. As a result, he's desperately determined to find a way of escape. It's not that he wants to rock anybody's boat or wreck anybody's day. It's just that he's a rebel to the wrong.

Some readers might be surprised to learn that there's a strong biblical basis for this kind of insurrection. It's true, of course, that the prophet Samuel likens rebellion to "the sin of witchcraft" (I Samuel 15:23) and that Paul advises believers in Jesus to submit to ruling authorities, even those who are godless and wicked (Romans 13:1-7; Titus 3:1). But these instructions, to be fully appreciated, have to be held in balance with the *other* side of the scriptural story: the side of Shadrach, Meshach, and Abednego, who told the King of Babylon, "We do not serve your gods, nor will we worship the gold image which you have set up" (Daniel 3:18); or Mordecai, the faithful Jew who refused to grovel before Haman, the arrogant Persian official (Esther 3:2); or Peter and the other apostles, who defied the high priest's order to stop preaching in Jesus' name, defending their actions with the words, "We ought to obey God rather than men" (Acts 5:29).

These figures inspire us with their unflinching courage. Each and every one of them stood firm, even under threat of death, against the unjust demands of overbearing, overstepping, usurping human rulers. They drew their strength from a single source. Like Robin Hood, they knew who the *true* King was, and they were uncompromising in their allegiance to Him. Like Asriel, they had strong feelings and convictions about the difference between good and evil, and they were resolved to side with the good at any cost. As loyal subjects of the right and the true, it only made sense that they should become rebels to the wrong.

There is, to be sure, a rather obvious problem with any comparison between Lord Asriel and these heroic biblical characters. *His* rebellion is directed specifically against *God.* From his perspective—and apparently from the perspective of the author who created him—God is the *real* culprit, the ultimate sponsor of chains, oppression, and injustice, the worst of all usurping tyrants. That's why Asriel isn't content to make war against the Church alone. He must take his quarrel straight to the doorstep of the Highest Power of all.

Is it possible to rebel against God and still be a rebel to the wrong? Therein lies the conundrum, the riddle of Lord Asriel, perhaps even the riddle of Philip Pullman himself. And it isn't as easy to resolve as some might suppose. For the answer to this question, as nineteenth-century author George MacDonald once wisely observed, is wrapped in contingencies. "Everything," as he put it, "depends on the kind of God one believes in."

> Instead of automatically blaming a person who does not believe in a God, we should ask first if his notion of God is a god that ought to be believed in.[8]

If it *isn't*—if, like Asriel, the individual in question sees God as a cruel dastard or a selfish tyrant—then it follows that he would be *wrong* to believe in Him or submit to His authority. It only stands to reason that a god who fits this description should be stiffly opposed and resisted. That, at least, is how MacDonald saw it. "I will accept no explanation of any way of God," he wrote, "that involves what I should scorn as false and unfair in a man"; for God to be God, He must be *more* than man, not less.[9] To repudiate an outrageous or defective deity is not to be a lawbreaker or a dangerous insubordinate. It's to be a rebel to the wrong.

The happy irony here is that rebels to the wrong who reject God on the basis of faulty notions of His character may sometimes end up serving His purposes and acknowledging His *true* nature in spite of themselves. Philip Pullman could be a case in point. Pullman has told us that, in his view, the most admirable and valuable people in the world are "those who do good things; no matter what they believe or don't believe, no matter what they feel."[10] He's right, of course; but not because faith doesn't matter or because the specific content of a person's faith is irrelevant. On the contrary, as the biblical writers affirm again and again, genuine belief is reflected in action. "Show me your faith without your works," says James, "and I will show you my faith by my works" (James 2:18). "Not everyone who says to Me, 'Lord, Lord,' shall enter the kingdom of heaven," declares Jesus, "but he who does the will of My Father in heaven" (Matthew 7:21).

Is it conceivable that Pullman, like Robin Hood and Lord

Asriel, is not so much a renegade to the truth as a rebel to the wrong? Could it be that in affirming freedom and justice and withstanding despotism and oppression he is actually paying tribute to the rightful King—the Lord of mercy, who is "gracious and full of compassion" (Psalm 111:4) and who comes to "proclaim liberty to the captives" (Isaiah 61:1)—whether Pullman knows it or not?

It's a definite possibility. Because, as George MacDonald so astutely pointed out, the rejection of false ideas about God is the indispensable and necessary "starting point toward discovering who God truly is."[11]

LIGHT
There can be no sin in resisting obvious evil.

> *"What you don't know is what the knife does on its own. Your intentions may be good. The knife has intentions, too."*
>
> —*The Amber Spyglass*, CHAPTER 14, "KNOW WHAT IT IS"

SORRY SCIENCE

His wounded hand throbbing, his head dizzy and spinning, Will reached out tentatively, groping for the lip of the window in the air. He sucked in his breath with astonishment, for it was just as Giacomo Paradisi had assured him—he could actually feel it! Closing his eyes, he ran his fingertips cautiously from one end of the seam to the other, pinching and squeezing the edges together. In the next instant the opening into the other world had completely vanished.

"Well done," said Giacomo softly. As the old man handed Will the knife's leather sheaf, he warned him to use the knife carefully. Some previous bearers had been careless, making windows between worlds that never should have been made. Others had forgotten to close what they had opened.

Will felt a chill go up his spine. Fingering the handle of the darkly glittering blade, he waited in silence for the old man to tell him more.

Giacomo explained that the alchemists and philosophers of the Guild—of which he was a member—were responsible for the Specters. Possessed with an overpowering desire for knowledge that could be used to further their own ends, the philosophers were constantly seeking to discover how a thing might be done, without ever asking themselves whether it *ought* to be done.

The knife Will was holding, he told them, was the key to their "success." Three hundred years before they had first unlocked its secrets. Three hundred years before the Specters had come. The quest for knowledge, he cautioned them, could be a perilous thing.

Lyra remembered a conversation she'd recently had down at the dock. A boy had told her about a man who, hundreds of years earlier, had cut lead into smaller and smaller pieces, hoping it would turn into gold. Eventually, the pieces were so small they couldn't be seen. Yet he kept cutting, and suddenly the Specters, who'd been folded and confined to that tiny space, rushed out. They'd been wreaking havoc ever since.

She shifted her attention back to Giacomo as he began

explaining the four rules of the knife to Will. After that, the old man had little more to say. His work was finished. "Now take the knife and go," he told Will hoarsely. "And may you use it more wisely than those who came before you."

* * * * *

Scientia. It's a little word with a big history—a *concept* that, in the process of time, has blossomed into a full-blown philosophy: the philosophy of science. But *scientia*, in the original Latin, was a humbler, less technical, more broadly suggestive term than its latter-day derivative. In its beginnings, it was merely the nominal form of the verb *scire*, "to know." To the average Roman on the street it meant knowledge, intelligence, understanding. As any careful reader must realize, these ideas are central to the story of *His Dark Materials*.

William Blake (1757–1827), the English metaphysical poet whose work has had such a profound influence on Pullman's imagination, wrote winsomely of the contrast between *innocence* and *experience*. That contrast can be summed up in a single word: *scientia.* Knowledge *is* the difference between Blake's Lamb, who is meek and mild, and his Tyger, whose eyes burn bright in the forests of the night. The Tyger is daunting for a very simple reason: It *knows* what the Lamb does not suspect.[1]

At its heart, the tale of Will and Lyra is a tale about the pursuit of *scientia.* It's an account of the journey from innocence to experience—a celebration of the process of growing up. Puberty, burgeoning sexuality, dawning "consciousness," the knowledge of good and evil—these are the themes that drive the narrative and give it its distinctive edge. At the epic's climactic moment, when "the two young people"[2] (no longer children) yield to their love for one another in an "Eden-like" glade, Pullman makes it clear that their act of passion has somehow become the salvation of the universe. Why? Because in succumbing to the "temptation" of sexual attraction, they have crossed the line between *innocence* and *experience*. They have laid hold of knowledge—*scientia*. And in Pullman's economy, it is knowledge that redeems the world and makes us fully human.

But the "carnal knowledge" of two young lovers isn't the only kind of *scientia* we find extolled in the story of *His Dark Materials*. Far from it. *Intelligence* is the great goal toward which everything strains in this vast and sweeping drama of men, angels, and elementary particles. Consciousness is the quality that makes the worlds go round. Understanding is the centerpiece of the drama. It's the coveted prize that Pullman's protagonists are seeking in their quest for dignity. It's also the forbidden fruit that the Authority and his minions are determined to withhold from them at any cost.

"All the history of human life," says Serafina Pekkala, "has been a struggle between wisdom and stupidity. . . . The rebel angels, the followers of wisdom, have always tried to open minds; the Authority and his churches have always tried to keep them closed."[3]

"There are two great powers," says John Parry, "and they've been fighting since time began."

Every advance in human life, every scrap of knowledge and wisdom and decency we have has been torn by one side from the teeth of the other. Every little increase in human freedom has been fought over ferociously between those who want us to know more and be wiser and stronger, and those who want us to obey and be humble and submit.[4]

Know more. Be wiser. Grow stronger. This, in a nutshell, is the philosophy of science, the creed of the technological age. Within the context of the drama these words ring out like a clarion call. The time has come, Pullman seems to say, for humanity to graduate from innocence to experience—to throw off the shackles of religiously imposed darkness and step into the light of open-minded investigation. Learn all you can learn. Question all you can question. Be all you can be. And pay no attention to those who want you to "obey and be humble and submit." A pathway to the stars lies open at your feet.

It's a heady message. Inspiring, stirring, ennobling. And yet, as even Pullman appears to realize, there *is* another side to the story.

KURT BRUNER and JIM WARE

That side emerges poignantly in the episode renarrated above, where Will is initiated as the bearer of the subtle knife. It's a painful initiation, from which he comes away wounded and bleeding. Nor is it complete until he's been issued a dire warning about the perils of the knife. For the subtle knife is capable of doing things its user neither intends nor understands. At times it appears to have a mind of its own. It can open a Pandora's box of unforeseen problems and complications. To wield it is to run an incalculable risk.

Case in point: The knife was invented, as Will's mentor, Giacomo Paradisi, explains, because "alchemists, philosophers, men of learning, were making an inquiry into the deepest nature of things." But as they pursued their investigations, pressing their experiments to the limits, tinkering with "the bonds that held the smallest particles of matter together," something happened that they did not have in mind. Something snapped at the heart of reality. The mysterious connections that hold the fabric of the universe together were compromised. As a result, the soul-devouring Specters of Indifference were loosed upon the world.[5]

Nor is this the full extent of the damage the knife has inflicted upon the cosmos. At the end of *The Amber Spyglass*, we learn that the subtle knife, by opening windows between the worlds, has cast a shadow of impending disaster over the entire universe. Through those windows, Dust, the life-giving stuff that arises "when matter begins to understand itself,"[6] is ebbing away at a steady and irreversible rate. If complete annihilation is to be averted, the openings will have to be shut. The knife itself will have to be destroyed.

That, of course, leads to the bitterest wound of all. For what this means for Will and Lyra, who are "melting with love" for one another, is that they must say good-bye. If they want to save creation, our young Romeo and Juliet must return to their respective worlds and close the doors behind them, never to meet again. It's an agonizing realization; When it dawns upon Will in all its fullness, he finds himself "gasping and shaking and crying aloud with more anger and pain than he [has] ever felt in his life."[7] In the end, he has reason to regret that he ever laid eyes on the subtle knife.

What exactly *is* this subtle knife? As with any piece of literary imagery, there's a sense in which this has to remain an open question; on one level, the knife simply "is what it is" within the context of the tale. But if Pullman's hints and clues are to be given any weight at all, on another level, the knife must represent something very specific indeed. In some way, this miraculous instrument, this tool that possesses the power to "kill God" by banishing the shadows of mystery and reducing reality to its smallest, most irreducible parts, must in fact *be* the knowledge—the *scientia*—that Asriel and his rebels are so desperately seeking. How interesting, then, that the subtle knife also has the potential to inflict terrible grief and damage upon the world.

The implication seems inescapable: Mankind is better off *without* some kinds of knowledge and some varieties of experience. There is, after all, something to be said for humility, obedience, and innocence.

This, whether Pullman realizes it or not, is the message of the biblical story of Eden. For the knowledge of good and evil that our first parents gained when they tasted the forbidden fruit was nothing but the pain of a broken relationship; it was simply the realization that "you don't know what you've got till it's gone."[8] As such, it was an experience they were never meant to have—a dreadful blow that left them "gasping and shaking and crying aloud with more anger and pain than [they] had ever felt in [their] lives." Clearly, the God whose words of prohibition and warning were calculated to spare them such anguish was no tyrannical despot. He was, on the contrary, a loving and caring Father, solicitous in every way for the welfare of His beloved children.

No wonder William Blake came to the realization that the transition from innocence to experience can be anything but an unmixed blessing. No wonder the *scientia* he gained as he traveled through this life led him to describe the day of his birth as a day of "Infant Sorrow."[9] But Blake knew that the story doesn't end there. As a Christian, Blake had glimpsed the hope that lies beyond the loss of innocence. He understood that paradise, once lost, can be regained. That's why he could conclude his *Songs of Innocence and Experience* with

this triumphant challenge to the Specters of sin, shame, and
mortality:

> *The Death of Jesus set me free:*
> *Then what have I to do with thee?*[10]

L I G H T

Some kinds of ignorance are bliss indeed.

"Liar! Liar!" the harpy was
screaming. "Liar!" . . .

She seemed to be screaming Lyra's
name, so that Lyra and liar were
one and the same thing.

—*The Amber Spyglass*, CHAPTER 21,
"THE HARPIES"

SILVERTONGUE

Weak and weary, her eyes still sore from weeping, Lyra stared
blankly at the dripping stone face of the great gray wall. Up
and up it towered into the eddying mist, its top completely
obscured in the opaque whiteness. She swallowed hard, trying desperately to drive the haunting image from her brain:
Pantalaimon, alone on the barren shore, disappearing into the
darkness behind her. Had she abandoned him for nothing?
Had she and Will come all this way only to be turned back
at the very door to the Land of the Dead?

She flinched as an earsplitting shriek split the air. A cloud of stench fell over her, causing her gorge to rise. Covering her mouth and nose, Lyra glared up at the squinting harpy perched on the ledge above her head. The foul creature pursed its horrible red lips in a grotesque human grimace, shook its filthy black wings, and hopped defiantly from one clawed foot to the other.

Will came up and stood beside her, jaw thrust forward, knife in hand, fearless as ever. But Lyra could see that even Will was at a loss. Even Will was tired and sore and discouraged. It was *her* turn to act, her turn to step into the gap. She wiped her eyes, lifted her head, and walked straight up to the harpy. She knew exactly what to do.

She asked the ugly creature her name—and how they could get her to open the door.

"No-name!" was the answer. "No deals either!" The creature paused and licked its dry, cracked lips. "Unless you can make me a good offer."

Lyra asked if she would let them through if she told the harpy a good story. The strange being dared her to try.

Lyra smiled slightly. A gush of pride and pleasure swelled her rib-cage as she promised to tell a story about all the strange adventures that had brought them here.

The harpy cocked an eyebrow and bent its head in her direction. Lyra moved a little closer. Now she was on familiar ground. Now her strength and confidence were returning in a flood-tide. Like her mother, the indomitable Mrs. Coulter, whom even the terrible Specters had to obey, Lyra knew she could manipulate any situation through the power of clever deception. Hadn't the kids in Oxford always swallowed her tall tales whole? Hadn't she won a kingdom for Iorek Byrnison with her artful falsehoods? Hadn't Iorek dubbed her *Silvertongue* in honor of the shining smoothness of her speech?

Iorek had strength, and Will had courage. But Lyra knew how to lie. It was her gift. It was her talent. It was her contribution to the cause. She'd lie for Roger. She'd lie for Will. She'd lie in the name of compassion and justice and all that was good and right.

Clasping her hands behind her back, Lyra promised to tell a fantastic tale of treasure and murder and shipwreck and spine-tingling, hair-raising escapes. She began by announcing that her parents, the Duke and Duchess of Abingdon, were very, *very* rich. She'd barely gotten into the story when the harpy was upon her, beating her with its wings, screeching and tearing at her scalp with sharp and bloody talons. Lyra covered her face and fell back with a cry.

"Liar! Liar!" screamed the indignant harpy.

* * * * *

Self-confidence can be a dangerous thing. The biblical maxim "Pride goes before destruction" (Proverbs 16:18) is more accurate as a description of day-to-day human experience than many of us are willing to admit. And the web of lies that you and I sometimes weave in a presumptuous attempt to promote self-interest really *does* have a way of catching up with us in the end. That's what Lyra discovered when she tried to bluff her way into the Land of the Dead.

Names, as we've already noted in the case of Lord Asriel, are important in the world of *His Dark Materials.* More often than not, the name of a major character reveals something vital about that person's temperament, outlook, and inward qualities. It's significant, then, that Philip Pullman, in interviews and public readings, has always made it clear that the name *Lyra* should be pronounced so that the first syllable sounds exactly like the word *lie.* That's because Lyra is a consummate liar.

Indeed, she's more than consummate. She's confident and proud. She's good at what she does, and she knows it. "I'm the best liar there ever was," she brags to Will.[1] She relies on her talent for bending the truth to extricate herself and her friends from all kinds of narrow scrapes and harrowing situations. As a result, her pride in this rare and precious gift becomes something more than mere preadolescent conceit. For Lyra, lying is actually a source of deep moral self-satisfaction. Stopping to reflect on her superiority as a fibber, she feels "warm and virtuous" inside.[2]

Nor is Lyra the only one who sees her penchant for prevarication in a positive light. "Deceptive, that's what you are, child," says Ma Costa, the gyptian boat-mother; and when Lyra seems taken aback, Ma clarifies her meaning by adding, "Can't you see I'm a paying you a compliment, you gosling?"[3] Will, who is obsessively honest, nevertheless admires Lyra's adroitness at spinning less-than-truthful yarns. He borrows a page from her book when he lies to the spying Gallivespians. Later he tells them, "If we deceived you, it was necessary."[4] King Iorek Byrnison, the great armored bear, memorializes Lyra's unparalleled achievement in hornswoggling his rival, the usurper Iofur Raknison, by giving her a new name. "You tricked Iofur Raknison?" he exclaims in admiration. "You are Lyra *Silvertongue*."[5]

At first glance, it would be easy to interpret this celebration of deception as a direct challenge to traditional morality and ethics. "Who says that lying is a vice?" Pullman seems to ask. "It ain't necessarily so. There may be occasions when lying is actually a virtue, situations where falsehood turns out to be a good and useful thing."

And on reflection, Christians might even be inclined to grant him the point. After all, didn't Rahab the prostitute lie to protect the Israelite spies? Didn't the Magi cover for the baby Jesus by giving Herod the slip and sneaking back to their own country by a different road? Didn't Corrie ten Boom deceive the Nazis in order to save Jewish lives?

But Pullman doesn't leave the question there. Instead, as the tale unfolds, he probes deeper, pushing the edges, hinting in one way and another that, deep down inside, even Lyra the liar knows that lying is inherently wrong. In so doing, he creates a powerful dramatic tension between two conflicting trajectories of moral thought.

Oh, the wicked liar, thinks Lyra as Mrs. Coulter tries to sell her a bill of goods about the purpose of the "experiments" at Bolvangar. *Oh, the shameless untruths she is telling!*[6] On discovering that the men of Trollesund have cheated Iorek Byrnison out of his armor, she comments, "I don't think that's right."[7] When she realizes that Lord Asriel has fooled her into betraying Roger, she reacts with white-hot righteous indignation: "She could have killed her father . . . for what he'd done to Roger. And to her: tricking her: how *dare* he?"[8] Clearly, Lyra possesses something that we might call an internal moral compass. And that compass is continually telling her that lying is not a good thing. At least it doesn't *feel* good when she and her friends are on the receiving end of the deception.

This is why, as the trilogy progresses, truthfulness becomes increasingly important to Lyra. As a matter of fact, it wouldn't be going too far to say that truth is the fulcrum upon which her entire story turns. She is, after all, a protégé with the alethiometer, the device that "measures truth." She's also passionate about keeping her word when she makes promises to friends like Roger and Will. As she travels from childhood to maturity, experiencing critical turning points along the way, she discovers that honesty and veracity are matters of the utmost importance in life, especially where relationships are concerned.[9] In the end, when her natural talent for reading the alethiometer deserts her, she makes up her mind to dedicate her life to the serious study of the instrument. In other words, she devotes herself to *the pursuit of truth.*[10]

It's in the scene narrated above that these apparently contradictory lines of development—the glorification of lies and the exaltation of the truth—come together with a resounding crash. And the collision occurs just at the moment when Lyra is feeling most confident about her prowess as a liar and most reassured about the goodness and usefulness of her ability to deceive. That's what makes the blow so shockingly memorable—and so lastingly instructive and beneficial.

Fresh from a successful stint of fabricating half-truths in the Suburbs of the Dead, Lyra launches into a repeat performance in an attempt to wheedle her way past the harpy who guards the entrance to the Underworld. But this time her well-worn stratagem doesn't work. This time the jig is up. Here, at the end of all things, in this world beyond all worlds where earthly veneers melt away and deceptions have no meaning, the harpy looks straight at Lyra and sees her for exactly what she is. And the harpy, in a burst of unexpected fury and violence, screams out her revelation for all to hear: *"Liar! Liar! Liar!"*

It's a moment of truth in the fullest and most meaningful sense of the phrase. For out of this conflict between honesty and deception—a conflict that has been brewing inside of Lyra ever since the story began—a clear message emerges: *Lying isn't all it's cracked up to be.* It's a rude awakening, and it brings Lyra to the end of herself at last:

> Will—I can't do it anymore—I can't do it! I can't tell lies! I thought it was so easy—but it didn't work—it's all I can do, and it doesn't work![11]

Is there a better way to learn this lesson than the way Lyra learned it? By finding out that, in the end, deception is a bad plan, not simply because an arbitrary "Authority" says so, but because it *just doesn't work*? Is there any more effective method of achieving genuine humility? of realizing that our human schemes and machinations are ultimately insufficient to deliver us from all our troubles? of discovering what it means to "miss the mark" and need a Savior?

"There is no creature hidden from His sight, but all things are naked and open to the eyes of Him to whom we must give account" (Hebrews 4:13). In other words, you can run—or lie—but you can't hide. This is why Solomon tells us (Rahab and Corrie ten Boom notwithstanding) that "lying lips are an abomination to the LORD" (Proverbs 12:22). This is why the psalmist declares that God will "cut off all flattering lips, and the tongue that speaks proud things, who have said, 'With our tongue we will prevail; our lips are our own; who is lord over us?'" (Psalm 12:3-4). For it is not the tongue of the deceiver but the words of the Lord that are "pure . . . like silver tried in a furnace of earth, purified seven times" (Psalm 12:6).

As a footnote, it's worth mentioning that, in spite of her fears to the contrary, lying *isn't* the only thing that Lyra can do. Another, better plan emerges once Will has used the knife to cut a way through into the Land of the Dead.

"Tell them the truth," he says to Lyra, as the ghosts of the captive souls gather around them. "We'll keep the harpies off."

LIGHT
To lie is to practice the art of self-deception.

"I wanted him to find no good in me, and he didn't. There is none. But I love Lyra."

—*The Amber Spyglass*, CHAPTER 31, "AUTHORITY'S END"

THE GREEN SHOOT

Marisa Coulter bit her lip and clutched the golden monkey to her breast. She could scarcely believe she'd made it to the Clouded Mountain. It was a marvel beyond comprehension: an outwardly rolling, inwardly spiraling, ever-shifting puzzle of shade and light. She took a step forward and glanced furtively along the shining corridor; then, her heart in her mouth, she slipped like a fleeting shadow down the vaulted galleries and up the pearly, nautilus-like stairways, worming her way relentlessly into the heart of the glowing fortress. All the while she was consumed with a single thought: *If I fail, Asriel's rebellion is in vain.*

She ordered the angel-sentinel before her to take her to the Lord Regent at once. And the angel, plainly stymied by her forthright speech, did as he was told.

At last she stood before him, covering her face with her arm, shielding her eyes from the brilliance of his presence: Metatron, Regent of the Authority, once Enoch, sixth from Adam, now Master of the Clouded Mountain and Lord of Angels. He wrapped himself in a veil of cloud and bent his fiery gaze upon her.

His flashing countenance was bearing down upon her with all the heat and intensity of the sun as he spoke, demanding to know whether she'd brought Lyra with her. Mrs. Coulter admitted she had not but promised to lead him to her.

Metatron hovered over her, his expression hot and fierce.

"Look at me, Lord Regent!" she said, digging her finger-nails into the palms of her hands to keep from crying out. "I know that nothing can remain hidden from you."

And he did. He leaned closer, and the air around her shimmered with the electricity of his nearness. She felt naked, exposed. Waves of shame, guilt, and remorse flooded over her as she stood beneath the probe of his ever-burning, all-seeing eye.

Presently he laughed. He described what he saw within her: Ambition and pride. A cold heart and a brutal mind. A soul devoid of compassion. A brain capable of conceiving unspeakable cruelties. Treachery, meanness, and lust for power. A cesspool of moral filth.

She squirmed. It was all true, every bit of it; and though she knew it to be true, it was torture to hear him say it. Only one thing consoled her: the desperate hope that her sins might be black enough and thick enough to hide the tender shoot of love that had sprouted in her heart—this deep and terrifying love for Lyra, her one and only child.

Even as she stood trembling before him, she could not help but marvel at the miracle of this love. Where had it come from? How had it had mastered her so completely? It was impossible to say. She knew only that it was there and that it had changed everything. She would risk everything now to protect her precious daughter. And this inescapable realization, as it enveloped and possessed her, was a source of both anguish and inexpressible joy.

"Yes," she whispered. "A cesspool of filth. And as such, more than capable of betraying the child and the man who fathered her." She moved a step closer. "Shall I take you to them now?"

* * * * *

When asked to name his favorite among the many compelling and carefully crafted characters inhabiting the world of *His Dark Materials*, Philip Pullman is ready with a surprising answer. He likes them all, he says, but he's quick to add that

Marisa Coulter is worthy of special notice. Mrs. Coulter, he explains, is a challenge to write. Why? Because "there's nothing she wouldn't do."[1]

And there isn't. As Pullman points out, she's "completely free of any moral constraint." In her relentless quest for power she remains consistently untrammeled by scruples of any kind. She seeks prestige through a loveless but politically advantageous marriage. When her husband, Edward Coulter, is killed as a direct result of her adulterous liaison with Lord Asriel, she turns to the Church as an even more promising avenue of self-advancement. In the process, she abandons Lyra, the unfortunate offspring of her illicit affair with Asriel. Even he is eventually relegated to the category of the expendable: When he no longer fits into her ambitious plans, she drops him in favor of the high-ranking Lord Boreal.

That's not all. In spite of her high-minded and grandiose aspirations, there's a side to Mrs. Coulter that can only be described as petty and mean. *She* is the one who comes up with the idea of kidnapping little children and cutting away their daemons. She even seems to derive a certain voyeuristic pleasure from witnessing the procedure—an assistant at Bolvangar describes her intense personal interest in the work as "ghoulish." She tortures prisoners, poisons Lord Boreal, and vows to destroy her own daughter rather than see the Church's agenda compromised. Her daemon, the diabolical golden monkey, displays a similar penchant for nastiness: He enjoys tormenting Pantalaimon and tearing the wings off bats.[2] All in all, it wouldn't be too much to say that Mrs. Coulter is a "paragon of evil." She really is capable of the most appalling behavior.

And yet there's another side to her story. For by the time she comes to the end of her long and tempestuous journey, Marisa has undergone a radical change. From a scheming political opportunist she has been transformed into a self-less servant—a heroine capable of foregoing personal ambition and sacrificing herself for the common good. More to the point, she has given up her dreams of domination and embraced the humblest, commonest, yet most important role any woman can ever assume—that of a dedicated mother. And this miraculous metamorphosis has been effected entirely by the power of love.

"A little green shoot" of love, she calls it. A tiny grain "no bigger than a mustard seed." It was planted during the days she spent with Lyra in a mountain cave high in a valley of perpetual rainbows. There she kept a lonely vigil, watching over the drugged and drowsing girl, feeding her broth and rice and tea, washing her face, changing her clothes, and combing her hot and sweaty hair.[3]

Marisa hardly knew what she was doing at the time. With every passing day she became more of a mystery to herself. She had promised to kill this child rather than allow the witches' prophecy concerning her to be fulfilled, and she knew that ruthlessness was essential to the success of her plan. But as the hours slipped away, and as she devoted herself to the mundane business of caring for Lyra's basic needs, her feelings began to shift. There came at length a moment when she could deny it no longer: She *loved* the sleeping girl. As she later explained it to Asriel, "The mustard seed had taken root and was growing, and the little green shoot was splitting my heart wide open."[4]

Pullman, then, is right. Mrs. Coulter is truly capable of *anything*—the good as well as the bad. That's why we find her so fascinating and engaging. In an important sense, she's just like you and me. And this, in a strange and paradoxical way, is an encouraging thought. For if her double-edged talent for the surprising and the unexpected extends so deeply into the realm of darkness, it must also stretch a long way into the regions of light.

Herein lies a mystery: the mystery and marvel of human nature. For the astonishing truth is that the creature possessing the most shocking potential for vileness is also the one with the greatest capacity for the sublime. The same being that, in a given situation, can so quickly become "a horror and a corruption" may, in another, emerge as something you might be "strongly tempted to worship."[5] This is what it means to be a man or a woman, a person created in God's image but fallen from grace. *This* is what it means to be a sinner in need of redeeming grace.

Mrs. Coulter came to feel that need intensely before the end. The weight of it lay heavily upon her when, having infiltrated the defenses of the Clouded Mountain, she stood at last before Metatron, Lord of Angels. In the heat of that encounter all of her pretenses were melted away. Her soul was laid bare beneath the insistent scrutiny of his flaming eye, and she had to admit that the bad elements far outweighed the good. She was forced to confess, if only to herself, that she was genuinely "corrupt and full of wickedness."[6]

This, given Pullman's views on sin and moral freedom, is a remarkable statement. But it's not the most noteworthy thing about Mrs. Coulter's response to Metatron's relentless probing. What *really* worried her in the crucible of that terrible moment was not the enormity of her guilt, but rather the possibility that Metatron would detect the tiny green shoot of love that had taken root in her heart.[7] She knew that if this love were discovered, the game would be over and her attempt to deceive the Lord Regent would fail. In that case, the rebel cause would be lost and her precious child, Lyra, would perish.

Her fears were well-grounded. For love, even the tiniest, seemingly most insignificant particle of it, is an unbelievably potent force. To control or conceal it is an extremely difficult proposition. Like a pinch of yeast in a lump of dough, it cannot stay hidden for long (Matthew 13:33). Like a seed planted in the ground, its inherent virtue will eventually assert itself whether we want it to or not; it sprouts and grows "by itself" (Greek *automate*, see Mark 4:26-29). To use a more contemporary analogy, it can be compared to a computer virus—a virus for *good*: once introduced into the system, it necessarily infects and reformats everything. For love, as the Scripture declares, is "strong as death . . . many waters cannot quench [it], nor can the floods drown it" (Song of Solomon 8:6-7).

Amor vincit omnia. "Love conquers all." It's a phrase that cynics and disillusioned sweethearts love to ridicule and lampoon. But that's because they haven't learned the difference between *amor* and *agape*. The *agape* love that saves the world—the love that God Himself *is* (I John 4:8)—is not the self-seeking, self-gratifying passion of impassioned paramours. On the contrary, it's the self-emptying, self-abnegating, other-centered attitude that says, "I would rather be accursed myself than allow you to come to harm" (see Romans 9:3). *This* is the potent and all-embracing love that Mrs. Coulter had to struggle so hard to keep hidden from Metatron. *This* is the love that compelled the Son of Man to "give His life a ransom for many" (Mark 10:45). Where it is present it will inevitably make itself known—in spite of all efforts to squelch or subdue it.

Ultimately, then, Mrs. Coulter's capacity for the unpredictable brought her to the most unexpected end of all: redemption through the power of love. In reflecting on her fate, it's

hard not to be reminded of another woman of ill repute—
that flagrant sinner who met Jesus in the house of Simon the
Pharisee and of whom the Savior said: "Her sins, which are
many, are forgiven, for she loved much" (Luke 7:47).

LIGHT

Sin and shame are no match for the power of love.

> *"I didn't know whether God had died, or whether there never had been a God at all. . . . And all that huge change came about as I had the marzipan in my mouth . . ."*
>
> —*The Amber Spyglass*, CHAPTER 33, "MARZIPAN"

KNOW WHO IT IS

Mary Malone lay back and settled herself comfortably on the thick carpet at the base of the tree, marveling again at the cookery and craftsmanship of the mulefa. Above her head the stars of that world, brighter and more numerous than those of her own, winked down through the glossy green leaves. At her side lay Will and Lyra, silent and expectant in the warm, fragrant night. Everything had grown very still; and in the stillness, the advice of the ghost—*tell them stories*—came back to her with fresh force. She propped herself on one elbow and resumed her narrative.

She'd been telling them about her past; how she'd always been fascinated by physics but at one time had also been a nun. Because of her scientific proclivities, the Church had allowed her to continue her university career.

Her life full, Mary had viewed the idea of being in love as something akin to going to China. People hear about China all their lives, but few ever expect to go there. Love, to her, was a distant, romantic mystery—something that *other people* experienced, but she never would.

One day, however, she was asked to give a paper on her research in Lisbon. Her lecture was well-received and, flushed with pleasure, Mary accepted an invitation to join her friends at a restaurant that evening. Before long she was deep in conversation with an Italian colleague sitting across from her. She found herself drawn in by his warmth and intellingence.

Sitting there with her friends in the twilight, surrounded by lemon trees and honeysuckle, savoring the sweet taste of marzipan on her tongue, she felt an unexpectedly pleasant and familiar feeling. She remembered that once, a long time before, a boy had danced with her at a party and kissed her lips and put marzipan in her mouth. She *had* known what it was like to be in love! And as she gazed across the table at her dark-haired, olive-skinned, brown-eyed Italian colleague, she knew that she wanted that experience again.

Lyra leaned forward eagerly, her eyes wide and bright.

Mary smiled and continued her story. She and the Italian

scientist had talked long into the night. They left the restaurant and walked together along the beach under the stars. It was a magical evening, with lights twinkling far out on the point and little waves lapping and hissing gently on the shore. He had a quiet way of talking and an easy laugh. Mary went barefoot and let her hair toss freely in the breeze, feeling happy and guilty and embarrassed by turns, hoping he'd think she was funny and pretty and smart.

And that's when another realization hit her. All at once she knew that this was a side of life she simply *couldn't* deny. *This* was what she wanted. Not confessions and creeds. Not dull prayers in an empty gray room. What did all *that* have to do with the simple joy of this enchanted moment? Nothing—nothing at all.

In that instant, she told Will and Lyra, something clicked in her mind and she knew exactly what she had to do. She put a hand to her breast and felt for the cross that hung there on a chain. Lifting her hair, she undid the clasp. She stood there for a moment, looking down at the crucifix in the palm of her hand, thinking about love, thinking about the taste of sweet almond paste. And then she reached back as far as she could and threw the thing into the sea.

And that, Mary concluded as she sat up and smoothed her skirt over her knees, was how she stopped being a nun. That's how she came to see that God doesn't exist and that Christianity was merely a powerful, convincing mistake.

* * * * *

Some decisions are too important to be made lightly. And some relationships are too vital to be entered into—or broken off—on a whim.

At a crucial point in the action of *The Amber Spyglass*, when the subtle knife has snagged and snapped and Will and Lyra are desperate to get it mended, Iorek Byrnison, armored bear and master smith, advises them to stop and think about what they're doing. As far as he's concerned, he tells them, it would be a mistake to repair the dangerous implement. But he's willing to help them as long as *they* are willing to do their homework and count the cost. "Know what it is that you're asking," he says, in a solemn, warning tone. "If you still want it then, I shall mend the knife."[1]

It would have been nice if Mary Malone had received the benefit of some similar counsel prior to making up her mind about the existence of God.

Mary, of course, is a scientist—a paragon of dispassionate rationality. That's why the mulefa, the wheel-riding creatures of *The Amber Spyglass*, are so anxious to enlist her help in solving the mystery of the dying wheel-pod trees. They trust her scientific instincts. They believe in her capacity to "see connections and possibilities and alternatives" that they themselves are unable to perceive.[2] They know that Mary is a logical thinker. How odd, then, that Mary, at a vital crossroads, seems to have made an important life decision on the basis of a classic non sequitur. How strange that, in that critical moment, her reasoning appears to have run something like this: *I like the taste of marzipan; I enjoy the feeling of being in love; therefore, there is no God.*

There's only one way to account for such sloppy syllogizing on the part of an otherwise intelligent and analytical mind: Something else must be going on below the surface. Some hidden element, unnoticed by the casual observer, must be muddying the waters. In Mary's case, that element isn't difficult to discern.

Mary is obviously proceeding on the basis of an assumption that Philip Pullman himself has articulated clearly and forcefully a number of occasions: namely, the idea that God is a killjoy and the Christian worldview is "essentially life-denying."[3] When she throws her crucifix into the sea, she is subscribing to the view that followers of Christ are basically dull-witted, sense-deprived bores who "spend years in solitary prayer, while all the joy of life [is] going to waste around [them]."[4] Like her literary creator, she is embracing Wendell W. Watters's cynical declaration that "the true Christian is running furiously on a treadmill to get away from whole segments of his or her human nature which he or she is taught to fear or about which he or she is taught to feel guilty."[5]

More particularly, Mary is giving credit to the shopworn notion that Christians see sin and sexuality as somehow synonymous—that there is, in fact, as Anne-Marie Bird observes, a "biblical connection between sexual awakening and the expulsion of 'man' from Eden."[6] This fallacy lies at the very heart of Pullman's trilogy. It's the principle that governs the "fixing" of daemons and explains the attraction of Dust to pubescent preteens. It's the reason Father Gomez can watch Will and Lyra strolling hand in hand under the trees with a firm conviction that they are "walking into mortal sin."[7] Most importantly, it's the basis of Pullman's contention that when the two young lovers finally embrace, they are somehow reliving the "original sin" of Mother Eve—and thus saving the world by reasserting mankind's bid for autonomy and independence.[8]

Given her presuppositions in this regard, it's no wonder that Mary opts out of her earlier decision to dedicate her life to Jesus.[9] She is, after all, a healthy young woman with healthy, normal hormones. She has vowed to become a nun, but she also enjoys being a girl, and she has just discovered that it's pleasant to laugh and talk with an attractive man under the leaves of the lemon tree in the lamplight of a summer evening. Why shouldn't she be offended at the thought of a God who creates people male and female and then denies them the pleasure of a kiss in the moonlight?

Unfortunately, the belief that God is opposed to sexuality and that believers have to "deny whole segments of their human nature" in order to qualify for His service isn't unique to Mary Malone. Nor did it originate with Philip Pullman or Wendell W. Watters. This subtle and pervasive error has been with us for a long, long time—at least since the New Testament era, when the apostle Paul found it necessary to denounce false teachers who went around forbidding marriage (see I Timothy 4:3) and creating a situation in which Christian couples had to be encouraged to "stop depriving one another" of normal marital relations (I Corinthians 7:5, NASB). Pullman's literary hero, John Milton, appears to have been countering a seventeenth-century version of this same "austere hypocrisy" when, in Book IV of *Paradise Lost*, he described Adam and Eve in their sinless, innocent state—*prior* to the Temptation and Fall—going to rest in their "inmost bower":

> *nor turned, I ween,*
> *Adam from his fair spouse, nor Eve the rites*
> *Mysterious of connubial bliss refused.*[10]

As Milton knew, there is no truth whatsoever to the claim that love, romance, and "connubial bliss"—if enjoyed within its appropriate context, the bond of marriage—are incompatible with spiritual purity and belief in God. No one who has ever read the Song of Solomon could possibly regard such a proposition with the slightest degree of seriousness. The fact of the matter is that God *likes* sexuality. It's a vital part of His plan for mankind's experience of the interpersonal *I and Thou*.

Chastity is a virtue not because sex is bad, but because sex, like fire or water, is a good but very powerful natural force that can do great damage if it isn't contained within the proper channels. Pullman, a responsible father of two sons and husband to the same woman since 1970, obviously understands this.

Nor is there any validity to the idea, so frequently referenced in *His Dark Materials*, that Christianity somehow disparages material pleasures and denies the value and significance of bodily life. The Scriptures plainly state that God Himself made the human body, along with the rest of the physical universe, and that when He had made them, He stepped back and declared them *good* (Genesis 1:31). He dignified the body even further by assuming human flesh in the person of Jesus Christ (John 1:14). And He "declared [Christ] to be the Son of God with power" by raising Him *bodily* from the dead (Romans 1:4). These teachings are fundamental to the biblical worldview. They are the ultimate motive for Christian charity and philanthropy; for as James so pointedly asks, what good does it do if we say to a needy brother or sister, "'Depart in peace, be warmed and filled,' but . . . do not give them the things which are needed for the *body*?" (James 2:16, emphasis ours). Clearly, our bodies occupy a vital place in the Creator's design for human life. That's why Paul urges us to present them to the Lord as "a living sacrifice, holy [and] acceptable to God" (Romans 12:1).

As for the body's *sensations*—its physical interactions with the enchanting barrage of sights, sounds, smells, and textures that ceaselessly assault our neurons as we make our way through this wondrous world—Paul boldly endorses them when he asserts that God "gives us richly all things to enjoy" (1 Timothy 6:17). The same perspective stands behind David's exultant and hopeful prayer: "You will show me the path of life; in Your presence is fullness of joy; at Your right hand are pleasures forevermore" (Psalm 16:11).

Mary, then, was tragically mistaken. As it turns out, she *could* have relished the taste of marzipan, savored the fragrance of lemons, thrilled to the kiss of a lover, *and* devoted herself to Jesus all at the same time. If only someone could have told her! If only she had bothered to find out exactly *whom* she was rejecting before taking the momentous step of throwing Him out of her life!

In that case, she might have been spared the embarrassment of basing her life on a logical fallacy. She might have avoided becoming the well-intentioned but sadly "solitary"[11] character who cuts such a lonely figure in *The Subtle Knife* and *The Amber Spyglass*. Instead of Malone—Mary, Alone[12]—she might have become Mary, daughter of the King and beloved of the eternal Bridegroom.

LIGHT
Don't reject what you don't understand.

*With a fast-beating heart, she
turned to him and said, "Will . . ."
And she lifted the fruit gently to
his mouth.*

—*The Amber Spyglass*, CHAPTER 35,
"OVER THE HILLS AND FAR AWAY"

EVE

Mary Malone could not shake her concern. Having spotted
a man she sensed carried malicious intent, she hated the idea
of Lyra and Will wandering unaccompanied into the forest to
search for their daemons. Caving to their insistence, however,
she packed them a meal and asked that they remain on the
prairie where a potential menace could be spotted from afar.

To reassure her, Will promised to use the knife and escape
into another world should they sense danger. Mary couldn't
argue. After all, both had faced and overcome much worse
peril in the past. But that was before she had become so
attached to them.

As they began their walk, Lyra and Will talked about whether they'd ever be able to return home. Lyra doubted she could return to Jordan College but said she wouldn't mind living with the gyptians.

Will wondered whether Lyra would want to live in Lord Asriel's world now that the great conflict had ended, but she reminded him that daemons can only live for a short time outside their own world. Her father's intentions would fail. His bravery and skill would ultimately be a waste.

Searching for daemons is no easy task, especially when one has no idea what form they might have taken. But Will and Lyra sensed shadows and movement just beyond, suggesting the daemons were nearby—perhaps edging closer as they gained confidence.

Walking on, Lyra asked Will about his plans. He must return home to be with his mother; he planned to look after her properly when he was grown and had his own place. Lyra thought it was unfair that a son should take take of his mom. Wasn't it supposed to work the other way around? And at some point, weren't sons supposed to move on with their own lives?

Refreshing themselves beside a bubbling stream, the two followed its flow deeper into the woods, finally sitting down to enjoy the meal Mary had kindly prepared.

Father Gomez, the man Mary had seen through the spyglass the prior evening, watched from the protective cover of a nearby bush. Without question, he knew that both were walking into mortal sin. He had to stop them. Gun in hand, he readied himself for the great task his destiny required. The priest had no desire to harm the boy, an innocent accomplice to the girl's evil purpose. But Lyra must die lest she damn the world once more as the first Eve had done. A single bullet from his rifle, and heaven would rejoice in his successful abortion of a second grand catastrophe for the race.

But before he could fix his target for a clean shot, something happened to interrupt his mission. A sudden and intense pain overtook Father Gomez as something grabbed hold of his daemon. He looked right, left, behind—but saw no one.

Moments later, the priest was dead, attacked by Balthamos before he could harm Lyra. The children, unaware of the close call or the heroic intervention of Will's old angelic friend, carried on as if nothing had happened.

As Will reclined on the blanket while eating some bread and cheese, Lyra felt a strange attraction. She had never noticed the feelings before. At least not such intense excitement. She reached into the basket and retrieved one of those little red fruits. With a fast-beating heart, she turned to him and called his name before lifting the fruit gently to his mouth.

The look in his eyes matched her own, and both felt an intoxicating rush of desire for the other. Before either knew how, their lips gently met.

"Just like Mary said," he breathed, "you know right away when you like someone."

"Oh, I love you, Will . . ." came Lyra's eager response as her nerves thrilled at his touch.

Kissing her repeatedly, Will found himself overwhelmed by the beauty of Lyra's fragrance, the touch of her hand, the taste of her mouth.

Safe from the deadly intentions of Father Gomez, alone in a place none could see, Lyra partook of forbidden fruit. A free choice made, her destiny fulfilled.

* * * * *

The 1998 film *Pleasantville* made a statement. It featured the very different lives of two siblings—brother and sister. The brother, the school nerd, spent every spare moment watching reruns of his favorite television show. Attracted to the ideal world it presented, the boy dreamed of one day living a life as perfect as those in the black-and-white paradise called Pleasantville.

The sister, on the other hand, liked real life. Attractive, cool, and popular with the boys—especially those she slept with—the last place on earth she would want to visit was that "goody-two-shoes" world her geeky brother idolized. She preferred life fast and loose, thank you very much.

As the story unfolds, both brother and sister end up stuck in Pleasantville, forced to live in a black-and-white world that knows nothing of color or the passion it symbolizes. That is, until the sister decides to educate them on how to really have fun!

Before long, teens begin having sex, women leave domineering husbands, and Mom exchanges a mundane marriage for the excitement of an extramarital affair. In short, people begin to experience what life beyond Pleasantville can be. In the process, their black-and-white world gradually fills with vibrant color.

Free from the constraints of moral restrictions, the residents of Pleasantville begin embracing the wonders and excitement of a passion they've never known. With the exception, that is, of a few stick-in-the-mud folks who want to get rid of the "coloreds" and return Pleasantville to the way it was. They like the world bland and predictable—as it should be! In the end, however, passion wins out and the entire community accepts color as something good.

Pleasantville's agenda could be summarized this way: "When we free people from the constraints of an outdated value system, they can discover the colorful world of passion. The problem with our culture is not those who promote freedom and sexual expression. The problem is those who would keep us from finding and fulfilling our desires."

There is just one problem with that message: It is the complete opposite of reality. Sin, not purity, robs life of passion and turns it into a bland and colorless existence.

The short-term thrill of illicit sex is quickly replaced by the guilt and inevitable consequences of leaving the protective parameters of innocence. Unfortunately, few in our generation comprehend the wonders of passion fulfilled within the context of purity, choosing instead to reject any limits on expression as things that steal enjoyment rather than increase its intensity.

Unfortunately, the new mythology Philip Pullman seeks to create in *His Dark Materials* involves a similarly backward assumption embodied in Lyra as she fulfills her prophesied role.

"There is a curious prophecy about this child," the witch told Lee Scoresby. "She is destined to bring about the end of destiny. But she must do so without knowing what she is doing, as if it were her nature and not her destiny to do it." [1]

What at first reading seems like nonsense evolves throughout the story, building anticipation for an unwitting role the girl will play in the rebellion against tyranny. You feel it when Lord Asriel reminds Lyra of Adam and Eve in the garden while trying to explain the concept of original sin, as if the ancient "fairy tale" foreshadows her own future. It shows up when a cleric tells Mrs. Coulter of a prophecy concerning her daughter, when Mary Malone learns from angels that she must "play the serpent" when Lyra somehow enters the new garden of Eden, and when Serafina Pekkala describes Lyra as a god destroyer—"the final weapon in the war against the Authority."[2]

Eventually, Mrs. Coulter tortures the witch Lena Feldt to discover her daughter's destiny—demanding to know Lyra's true identity.

> "She will be the mother—she will be life—mother—she will disobey—she will—"
>
> "Name her! You are saying everything but the most important thing! Name her!" cried Mrs. Coulter.
>
> "Eve! Mother of all! Eve, again! Mother Eve!"[3]

Lyra does not play the part of a battling warrior charging God's fortress but the new Eve who will free all worlds from the grey existence of submissive obedience, infusing the "color" of passionate autonomy into the universe. In short, she serves Pullman's vision of changing "original sin" from mankind's terrible downfall to its great liberation.

"At the core of *His Dark Materials*," write Lance Parkin and Mark Jones in their guide to Pullman's trilogy, "is a radically different interpretation of the Fall. Philip Pullman argues that the Fall was a necessary and desirable stage in the evolution of humankind. The loss of innocence was necessary for humans to acquire wisdom. . . . The fixing of one's daemon symbolizes that moment in life when one passes from a state of innocence—or ignorance as Pullman would say—to a state of experience and knowledge. Pullman therefore fundamentally opposes the notion of original sin, rejecting outright that the Fall was anything other than essential."[4]

The rebels of *His Dark Materials* are the good guys who want to open minds toward wisdom and experience in opposition to those loyal to the Authority who seek to keep people innocent and submissive. This central conflict of *His Dark Materials* culminates with two equally significant and interdependent scenes: first, the climactic battle between Asriel's army and the Authority's forces; second, the moment of temptation when Lyra—the new Eve—makes a fateful choice to leave the "ignorance" of innocence for the "knowledge" of experience, both symbolized by the inference of sex with Will. These dual events become the two-edged sword used to kill "God" once and for all. In the process, Pullman replaces the "Kingdom of Heaven" and its sovereign monarch with the "Republic of Heaven" in which citizens rule their own lives by throwing off any form of "destiny" or restrictions tyranny might impose.

Unfortunately, Pullman's stories turn reality on its head. Like the movie *Pleasantville*, he offers an alternative mythology that fails to ring true because it misperceives and misrepresents the Christian view of what took place in Eden.

Imagine everything you could ever want being placed before you with the invitation to enjoy it all. You may partake as much, as often, and as long as you like. No guilt. No calories. No limits—except one. The only concession on your part is to stay away from one tree with a particular type of fruit. Anything and everything in the world in exchange for one restriction. Who wouldn't jump at such a deal? Adam was given the chance.

And the LORD God commanded the man, saying, "Of every tree of the garden you may freely eat; but of the tree of the knowledge of good and evil you shall not eat, for in the day that you eat of it you shall surely die." (GENESIS 2:16-17)

Why would God place something in the garden that He didn't want Adam and Eve to experience? If Eden was a gift to be enjoyed and managed by them, why include something that might be harmful? It was not as if God had to include the tree. Couldn't He have just left it out of the garden to avoid problems?

God made mankind to be His bride—someone with whom He could have a mutually chosen relationship. The tree was a symbol of Adam's freedom to accept or reject God's offer of intimacy. The tree was not placed in the garden to tempt but to testify. It stood as a symbol, a daily reminder to Adam and Eve that they could enjoy God's loving protection or chart their own course. The choice was made clear and the consequences explained. It was not necessarily the fruit from the tree that was harmful, but what it represented.

If there had been no tree, there would have been no choice.

Had there been no freedom to choose, there could have been no real love. In the words of Milton's *Paradise Lost*, Adam and Eve were

> *Sufficient to have stood, though free to fall. . . .*
> *Not free, what proof could they have giv'n sincere,*
> *Of true allegiance, Constant Faith or Love?*[5]

Adam, our representative, was given a choice that would determine the course of all human history (I Corinthians 15:22). That choice was made each time he walked past the fruit hanging from a tree that could give knowledge beyond innocence—and experiences beyond the rich adventure life was made to be.

What is freedom? To many, inspired by Lucifer's rebellion, it is rejecting all forms of authority— becoming master of your own destiny, god of your own life. But there is a catch. With rejection of God-ordained authority comes slavery to your own passions and limitations. No longer able to choose the good, those who've chosen such "freedom" are left with nothing but the marred scraps of evil.

True freedom is the ability to choose from the countless good gifts of God that He created for us to experience without guilt or consequence. Unspoiled by rebellion against beauty and goodness, we remain free to enjoy pleasures made for deep fulfillment rather than empty enslavement.

SHEDDING LIGHT
on *His Dark Materials*

Lyra, like Adam and Eve, did us no favors by accepting the serpent's invitation to knowledge beyond innocence. You see, when we turn our back on the good that God is, all that remains is the bad He is not.

LIGHT
Obedience frees us from the slavery of sin.

Things fall apart; the centre cannot hold . . .

—WILLIAM BUTLER YEATS, *The Second Coming*

THE MISSING PIECE

Afterthoughts

"*The Golden Compass?*" said my friend, picking up the battered paperback that lay atop the perennial pile of papers on my desk.

"Yes," I responded, glancing up briefly. "Part One of *His Dark Materials*. It's a trilogy by Philip Pullman. One of the most popular juvenile fantasies to be published in the last ten years—possibly in the past half century. Winner of the Whitbread Award and the Carnegie Medal. Soon to be a big-budget New Line Cinema film. Kurt Bruner and I are doing a book on it."

"*Pullman*," he mused, almost as if trying to put a face to the name. "Pretty dark stuff, huh?"

THE AUTHOR IN SPITE OF HIMSELF

I've given that last question a lot of thought during the weeks and months since Kurt and I first undertook this project. And the more I've pondered it, the more certain I've become that my friend was wrong. As a matter of fact, I'm now of the firm opinion that the world of *His Dark Materials* isn't particularly "dark" at all.

That's not for lack of trying on the author's part, of course. Pullman definitely deserves an A for effort. He's done his level best to offend the sensibilities of traditionally minded, God-fearing people. He's demonized the Church, castigated Christianity, and even made a bid at "killing God." He's cast a shroud of uncertainty over established standards of morality and truth, transforming "villains" like Lord Asriel and Mrs. Coulter into inspiring heroes, creating a winsome protagonist whose greatest virtue is her penchant for lying, and challenging our notions of right and wrong with statements like "A murderer [is] a worthy companion."[1]

Yet despite the shadows that hang about the perimeter of his imaginary world, Pullman hasn't quite succeeded in keeping out the light. It seeps in relentlessly through the cracks.

It upstages the writer's purported agenda and steals the scene at every opportunity. And it makes its presence felt most effectively at the very heart of the drama.

There's an important reason for this. Pullman, as we've had ample occasion to note, isn't quite comfortable with the implications of his own godless philosophy. At the end of the day, he can't accept the implications of his superficially relativistic ethic, nor does he feel truly at home in an impersonal universe composed solely of particles and Dust. He believes in goodness, beauty, and truth. And as is always the case with a skilled storyteller, his best thoughts and feelings come through in the telling of his tale.

That's why Lyra, the consummate liar, eventually has to face the fact that truth is her only viable option. That's why Will, the strong, self-reliant hero, is forced to admit his need for companionship, assistance, and grace. That's why Mary, the atheistic rationalist, feels such a desperate need for purposeful "connection" with the rest of the universe.[2] That's why Pullman himself, who openly criticizes J. R. R. Tolkien's "escapism" and tells us that this physical universe is our "only home,"[3] so obviously delights in the invention and exploration of other worlds. Whether he wants to admit it or not, he *knows* there must be something better "out there"—something more perfectly suited to the highest aspirations of the human heart.

As it turns out, then, there's a remarkable lack of "darkness" about the world of *His Dark Materials*—remarkable in view of the author's apparently amoral and atheistic intentions. Contrary to my friend's expectations, this is *not* a universe rife with demonic wickedness. Instead, it's shot through from end to end with shafts of strangely conspicuous light. It's a world where the act of "offering eager obedience to a stronger power that [is] wholly right" can be called by its rightful name: *the strangest of pleasures.*[4] It's a place where genuine *authority*, a dirty word when applied to God or the Church, is nevertheless the distinguishing mark of wise and effective leaders like John Faa and Farder Coram.[5] It's a breathtaking field of wonders where the glories of the Aurora Borealis can be so piercingly beautiful that they strike the beholder as being "almost holy."[6]

Most importantly, this is a world dominated by its creator's keen sense of the centrality of personality and relationship—a place where only the hope of *I and Thou* can reconcile an honest man like Lee Scoresby to the prospect of spending eternity as a mass of floating particles. "There'll be all the time in the world," says Lee's ghost in a heroic attempt to put a good face on the idea of disembodied oblivion, "to drift along the wind and find the atoms that used to be Hester, and my mother in the sagelands, and my sweethearts."[7] *Anything* is tolerable, Scoresby seems to say, as long as you've got somebody to share it with.

In light of all this, it's not surprising that Tony Watkins

says many of Pullman's values "are quite consistent with a Christian worldview."[8] It's no wonder he adds that Pullman, "unlike many contemporary writers, . . . is not a moral relativist."[9] Nor is it strange that Pullman can label himself "a Christian atheist."[10] As Kurt so aptly expresses in his introduction to this volume, the author of *His Dark Materials* is standing very near the lamp. The only problem is that he has his back to the light.

ECHOES IN THE SPACES

It's possible to characterize this paradox, this striking inconsistency between superstructure and foundation within Pullman's invented universe, in a couple of different ways. Either the world of *His Dark Materials* is a raging storm of antitheistic rebellion swirling around a peaceful eye of Christian presuppositions, or else it's a galaxy of glowing spiritual and moral truths clustered about an empty black hole. However you look at it, there's a missing piece at the heart of the grand design—a dissonant note in the middle of the symphonic structure. The details of the story don't match the motives that are supposed to be driving the action.

Why should this be so? I'd suggest that it's because Pullman, like Mary Malone, is *missing God* in the worst way. Having rejected the faith of his childhood—the faith of his beloved grandfather Sidney Merrifield, the English vicar who did so much to guide young Philip's moral development and shape his spiritual outlook—he's left with nothing but dis-connected fragments of the worldview that once impacted his thought so profoundly. He feels sharply the presence of Sartre's "God-shaped hole" at the center of his conscious-ness.[11] It's even possible to argue that this "hole" is the over-arching and unifying theme of his great epic fantasy. As a matter of fact, it wouldn't be stretching a point to say that Pullman's tale is *all about* his desire for God—if only in a negative and inverted sense.

He has practically told us so himself. In his 2002 May Hill Arbuthnot Honor Lecture, Pullman spoke at length about an "attitude" that underlies everything he writes:

> I suppose I could describe it as coming to terms with an absence—the absence of God—because I cannot believe in the God who is described by churches and in holy books. So I'm conscious of God only as an absence, but an absence which is full of echoes, trou-bling echoes and unhappy ones, consoling echoes and kindly ones, chastening ones and wise ones. . . . Echoes in the space where God has been.[12]

FATHER HUNGER

Perhaps this yearning for "the God who is no longer there"— this nostalgic straining after the echoes in the spaces—is reflected most poignantly in the role Pullman assigns to fatherhood, father figures, and father-child relationships in the story of *His Dark Materials*.

As we noted in the chapter entitled "Family," fathers tend to be conspicuously missing from the action of this tale. Like Pullman's God, we are conscious of them primarily "as an absence." Will, when we first meet him, knows his dad only as a boy knows a hero in a book: as an adventurer in faraway lands, a face in an old photograph, an inspiring but semilegendary figure. Lyra's father, on the other hand, is present but detached: a cold and distant man who lets his daughter down so thoroughly and completely that she is eventually driven to cry out, "You en't human, Lord Asriel. You en't my *father*. My *father* wouldn't treat me like that."[13]

And yet for all this, the importance of fathers—their love, their protection, their authority, their guidance—is underscored again and again throughout the three novels. This emphasis is expressed not only *negatively*—in troubling and chastening "echoes," but *positively*—through powerful portraits of father figures who behave as fathers are supposed to behave and do what fathers are supposed to do.

Thus it happens that Will *does* eventually get the chance to meet John Parry and "take up his father's mantle"; and while this encounter is both terrifying and tragic, it also proves to be the experience that affirms Will in his young manhood and pushes him over the border between childhood and adolescence.[14] In the end, Will even receives the words of love, approval, and affirmation that we all long to hear from our dads: "Well done, my boy. Well done indeed."[15]

As for Lyra, everything she has missed in her relationship with Asriel is made up to her in double measure when she falls into the hands of the gyptians of the Eastern Fens. For her, John Faa, the gyptian king, is all that a father ought to be—and more. Upon entering the presence of this "stern and massive" figure for the very first time, the usually cocksure Lyra reacts with fear, "and what she was most afraid of was his kindness."[16] When she stands trembling before him, smitten in conscience and fully expecting to be reprimanded for past misdeeds, she is granted *grace* instead: "We en't going to punish you," says the formidable old man with a reassuring smile.[17] In scenes like these, Lyra discovers what Pullman later states for us in the most straightforward language: "John Faa was a shelter and a strong refuge"[18]—the kind of shelter and refuge every child wants in a dad.

Then there's Farder Coram: the elderly sage who serves as John Faa's right-hand man—the "seer" who hovers over Lyra, guiding and protecting her with supernatural wisdom and solicitous care. To him Pullman attributes an inborn authority and a benevolent omniscience that are all but astonishing in the context of a tale that encourages us to question the motives of "those who want us to obey and be humble and submit."

"All your doings," John Faa tells Lyra, "they all get back to

Farder Coram here."[19] The implication is clear: Farder Coram knows all about you. He wants you to do the right thing. But he loves you just as you are. Even his name carries hints of the significance of his character: the title *Farder* is apparently a "Fen-Dutch" form of the word *father*, and *Coram* comes directly from a Latin phrase that has long been a standard part of the theologian's working vocabulary: *Coram Deo*—"in the presence of God."

Negligent and absentee parents notwithstanding, then, fathers play a vital role in the drama of *His Dark Materials*. Fatherhood matters to Philip Pullman, and he does a masterful job of showing us exactly what it should look like in the characters of John Faa and Farder Coram. He plainly understands the deepest yearning of the human heart: the desire for a long-suffering, all-knowing, all-powerful Abba who never slumbers or sleeps—a "Daddy" to whom we can always turn when we need "a shelter and a refuge."

"I'D LOVE TO MEET HIM"

What makes this picture all the more intriguing is the distinctive coloring it assumes in light of Philip Pullman's relationship with his own dad.

For most of his life, Pullman believed that his father, Alfred Outram Pullman, a dashing RAF pilot, had met his end while fighting Mau Mau terrorists in Kenya in 1953. Young Philip, who was seven at the time, never had an opportunity to know his dad in an intimate, personal way. He was aware of him only as a glamorous war hero.

That in itself might not have been so bad. But in later life, our author discovered that the circumstances surrounding his venerable parent's death were not quite as honorable as he had supposed. As it turned out, Alfred had *not* perished in the heat of battle. In actuality, he had crashed while flying under the influence of alcohol, practicing maneuvers for an upcoming air display. There was even an indication that his drunkenness—and the accident—may have been intentional. Alfred, it seems, had been struggling with a host of personal problems, including extramarital affairs and an impending divorce.

Pullman's response to this disturbing revelation is deeply affecting:

> So all my life I've had the idea that my father was a hero cut down in his prime, a warrior, a man of shining glamour, and none of it was true. Sometimes I think he's really still alive somewhere, in hiding, with a different name. I'd love to meet him.[20]

Tony Watkins comments, "In *The Subtle Knife*, Will is also preoccupied with the heroic father he had never known. Could something of Philip Pullman's own deep—even subconscious—longings be expressing themselves in Will's search for his father?"[21]

It's an excellent question. But I have a feeling that it doesn't probe deeply enough. For my part, I can't help wondering: Could Pullman's frustrated yearnings for an earthly father have anything to do with his confused, ambivalent, and self-contradictory attitude toward God? Is it his profound, if subliminal, disappointment with his earthly dad that drives him to repudiate his heavenly Father so fiercely and outspokenly? Does he "miss God" in the same way he misses his father? Could he be telling us that he'd like to meet *Him*, too? I think it's a possibility worth pondering.

THE HUB OF THE WHEEL

By now my point should be obvious: The "missing piece" at the heart of *His Dark Materials* is God Himself, the heavenly Father Pullman has never known. In the end, *He* is the only possible source of the light that pervades this grand and luminous world. *He* is the single center of gravity that can bring cohesiveness and integrity to Pullman's sometimes brilliant but often muddled configuration of moral and spiritual truths. He alone can tell us why lying is bad, kindness is good,[22] holiness is beautiful, grace is essential, and personal relationship is indispensable to the meaning of human existence. Without Him there is no basis for supposing that innocent children ought to be rescued from villains like the Gobblers or that judgment, wrath, and retribution should be visited upon the "infernal wickedness" of agencies like the Oblation Board.[23] Ultimately, He is the one "reason for doing good"[24] that any man or woman can ever have. Dust, for all its attractive features, is an inadequate substitute. For Dust, however personal and conscious it may be, can never become "a shelter and a refuge" for anybody. It can never smile and say, "Well done, my boy."

Only a personal Creator-God can do that. And not just *any* personal Creator-God. The one God who will suffice is "the God and Father of our *Lord Jesus Christ*" (Ephesians 1:3, emphasis ours). For it is only in *Christ*—the person most conspicuously absent from all the God-talk we encounter in *His Dark Materials*—that we are able to grasp what the Father is really like. "No one has seen God at any time," says the apostle John. "The only begotten Son, who is in the bosom of the Father, He has declared Him" (John 1:18). In Christ the scattered pieces of the puzzle come together in a meaningful pattern at last. In Him the spokes fit snugly into the hub of the wheel:

For by Him all things were created, both in the heavens and on earth, visible and invisible, whether thrones or dominions or rulers or authorities— all things have been created through Him and for Him. He is before all things, and in Him all things hold together. (COLOSSIANS 1:16-17, NASB)

Without Him, the center cannot hold.

Jim Ware

Endnotes

1. Videotaped interview with Philip Pullman featured on Stagework.org © 2006/07 The Royal National Theatre. All rights reserved. Video last accessed 4/4/07 at http://www.stagework.org.uk/webdav/servlet/harmonise?Page/@id=6005&Session/@id=D_Ntrh0ktwfPStOA6CPrLq&Section/@id=62

2. Ibid.

Chapter 1: Other Worlds

The authors' imaginative adaptation to begin the chapter is based on pages 16–26 of The Golden Compass.

1. J. R. R. Tolkien, *The Tolkien Reader*, ed. Christopher Tolkien (New York: Ballantine Books, 1966), 74–75.

2. Ibid.

3. Philip Pullman, *The Golden Compass* (New York: Dell-Laurel Leaf, an imprint of Random House Children's Books, a division of Random House, Inc., 1995), 330.

4. Tolkien, *Tolkien Reader*, 74–75.

Chapter 2: Daemons

The authors' imaginative adaptation to begin the chapter is based on pages 146–147 of The Golden Compass.

1. Tony Watkins, *Dark Matter: Shedding Light on Philip Pullman's*

Trilogy His Dark Materials (Downers Grove, IL: InterVarsity Press, 2004), 136.

2. Philip Pullman, *The Subtle Knife* (New York: Dell-Laurel Leaf, an imprint of Random House Children's Books, a division of Random House, Inc., 1997), 18.

3. http://www.allaboutturkey.com/sozlukmit1.htm, last accessed 4/20/07.

4. C. S. Lewis, *The Discarded Image: An Introduction to Medieval and Renaissance Literature* (Cambridge: Cambridge University Press, 1964, 2003 edition), 40–41.

5. John Milton, *Paradise Lost & Paradise Regained*, bk. 3, ed. Christopher Ricks (New York: Signet Classic, 2001), lines 461–462.

6. Lewis, *The Discarded Image*, 40–41.

7. Pullman, *The Golden Compass*, 172.

8. Ibid., 241 (Authors' emphasis).

9. Ibid., 248.

10. Millicent Lenz and Carole Scott, ed., *His Dark Materials Illuminated: Critical Essays on Philip Pullman's Trilogy* (Detroit: Wayne State University Press, 2005), 45.

Chapter 3: "I and Thou"

The authors' imaginative adaptation to begin the chapter is based on pages 185–188 of The Golden Compass.

1. Lenz and Scott, ed., *His Dark Materials Illuminated*, 210, note 10.

2. Martin Buber, *I and Thou*, tr. Walter Kaufman (New York: Touchstone/Simon and Schuster, 1996).

3. Martin Buber, *Good and Evil*, tr. Ronald Gregor Smith and Michael Bulock (Upper Saddle River, NJ: Prentice Hall, 1997), 88.

4. John Donne, "Holy Sonnets, V" in *John Donne: Selected Poems*, ed. John Hayward (New York: Viking Penguin, 1950), 167.

5. *Conscientia* (Latin); *syneidesis* (Greek).

6. Pullman, *The Golden Compass*, 191.

7. Buber, *I and Thou*, 112.

Chapter 4: Dust

The authors' imaginative adaptation to begin the chapter is based on pages 243–250 of The Golden Compass.

1. http://en.wikipedia.org/wiki/Dark_matter

2. John Gribbin and Mary Gribbin, *The Science of Philip Pullman's His Dark Materials* (New York: Alfred A. Knopf, 2005), 27.

3. http://www.philosophypages.com/ph/spin.htm

4. Anne-Marie Bird, "Circumventing the Grand Narrative: Dust as an Alternative Theological Vision in Pullman's *His Dark Materials*" in *His Dark Materials Illuminated*, 191.

5. *Paradise Lost & Paradise Regained*, bk. 2, lines 910–916.

Chapter 5: Family

The authors' imaginative adaptation to begin the chapter is based on pages 343–346 of The Golden Compass.

1. Pullman, *The Golden Compass*, 16–17.

2. Paul Vitz, *Faith of the Fatherless* (Dallas: Spence, 1999), 5.

Chapter 6: Will and Grace

The authors' imaginative adaptation to begin the chapter is based on pages 2–4 of The Subtle Knife.

1. http://www.textualities.net/writers/features-n-z/ pullmanp01.php, under the question "Tell me about the alethiometer."
2. Philip Pullman, *The Amber Spyglass* (New York: Dell-Laurel Leaf, an imprint of Random House Children's Books, a division of Random House, Inc., 2000), 440.
3. *Invictus*, William Ernest Henley, 1849–1903.
4. Pullman, *The Amber Spyglass*, 444.
5. Pullman, *The Subtle Knife*, 161.
6. Ibid., 279.
7. Ibid., 272.
8. Pullman, *The Amber Spyglass*, 398.
9. Ibid., 399.
10. Ibid., 404.
11. "How Can I Keep From Singing?" was written by American Baptist minister Robert Wadsworth Lowry in 1860. Others credit it as a traditional Quaker hymn.
12. Pullman, *The Amber Spyglass*, 458.

Chapter 7: Angels

The authors' imaginative adaptation to begin the chapter is based on pages 114–125 of The Subtle Knife.

1. 2 Kings 6:17, (NIV).

2. Pullman, *The Amber Spyglass*, 356.

3. Ibid., 356–357.

Chapter 8: The Authority

The authors' imaginative adaptation to begin the chapter is based on pages 24–29 of The Amber Spyglass.

1. Mark Rutland, *Behind the Glittering Mask* (Ann Arbor, MI: Servant Publications, 1996), 20.

2. Pullman, *The Subtle Knife*, 41.

3. Ibid., 240–242.

4. Pullman, *The Amber Spyglass*, 186.

5. Ibid., 293–294.

6. *Behind the Glittering Mask*, 20–21.

7. Pullman, *The Amber Spyglass*, 28.

8. Milton, *Paradise Lost & Paradise Regained*, bk. 5, lines 852–861.

9. Rutland, *Behind the Glittering Mask*, 47.

Chapter 9: Magisterium

The authors' imaginative adaptation to begin the chapter is based on page 68 of The Amber Spyglass.

1. As of this writing, director Chris Weitz and the executive staff of New Line Cinema have announced their intentions of removing the "anti-religious" overtones of Pullman's battle against "an evil, all-powerful church" from the film version of *The Golden Compass*. We're curious to see if this can be managed without doing irreparable

damage to the original story. (Source: www.scifi.com/
scifiwire/art-main/html?2004-12/10/10.00.film).

2. Pullman, *The Subtle Knife*, 44–45.

3. Pullman, *The Golden Compass*, 113.

4. Pullman, *The Subtle Knife*, 40.

5. Ibid., 190.

6. Pullman, *The Amber Spyglass*, 393.

7. Pullman, *The Subtle Knife*, 34.

8. From *The Amber Spyglass*, chapter 6, "Preemptive Absolution,"
59–68.

9. Pullman, *The Golden Compass*, 27.

10. Latin *magister* can mean either "master" or "teacher." Thus,
the teaching hierarchy of the Roman Catholic Church is also
known as the *Magisterium*.

11. Andrew Leet, "Rediscovering Faith through Science Fiction:
Pullman's *His Dark Materials*," in *His Dark Materials Illuminated:
Critical Essays on Philip Pullman's Trilogy*, ed. Millicent Lenz with
Carole Scott (Detroit: Wayne State University Press, 2005),
176.

12. Quoted in Tony Watkins, *Dark Matter*, 20.

Chapter 10: Rebel to the Wrong

*The authors' imaginative adaptation to begin the chapter is based on pages
334–337 of* The Amber Spyglass.

1. With acknowledgments to Dennis Agajanian, *Rebel to the Wrong*
(Light Records, 1981).

2. Pullman, *The Subtle Knife*, 41.

3. Ibid., 240.

4. Burton Hatlen, "Pullman's *His Dark Materials*, A Challenge to the Fantasies of J. R. R. Tolkien and C. S. Lewis," in Lenz and Scott, *His Dark Materials Illuminated*, 88.

5. Parkin and Jones, *Dark Matters*, 95.

6. Aleph, samekh, and resh are the Hebrew letters transliterated as *sr*.

7. Pullman, *The Golden Compass*, 12.

8. George MacDonald, *Discovering the Character of God*, ed. Michael R. Phillips (Minneapolis: Bethany House Publishers, 1989), 19.

9. MacDonald, *Discovering the Character of God*, 249.

10. From Pullman's Arbuthnot Lecture; quoted in Lenz and Scott, *His Dark Materials Illustrated*, 11.

11. MacDonald, *Discovering the Character of God*, 19.

Chapter 11: Sorry Science

The authors' imaginative adaptation to begin the chapter is based on pages 129–130 and 160–166 of The Subtle Knife.

1. William Blake, "The Tyger," in *Songs of Experience. The Poetry and Prose of William Blake*, ed. Geoffrey Keynes (New York: Random House, 1927), 73–74. Both "The Tyger" and "The Lamb" appear in this classic collection of poems first released in 1794.

2. Pullman, *The Amber Spyglass*, 414.

3. Ibid., 429.

4. Pullman, *The Subtle Knife*, 283.

5. Ibid., 165.

6. Pullman, *The Amber Spyglass*, 28.

7. Ibid., 442.

8. Joni Mitchell, "Big Yellow Taxi," © Siquomb Publishing Co. BMI, 1966–69.

9. Blake, "Infant Sorrow," in *Songs of Experience. The Poetry and Prose of William Blake*, 77.

10. "To Tirzah;" Ibid., 80.

Chapter 12: Silvertongue

The authors' imaginative adaptation to begin the chapter is based on pages 256–261 of The Amber Spyglass.

1. Pullman, *The Subtle Knife*, 91.

2. Pullman, *The Amber Spyglass*, 152.

3. Pullman, *The Golden Compass*, 100.

4. Pullman, *The Amber Spyglass*, 159.

5. Pullman, *The Golden Compass*, 305, italics added.

6. Ibid., 248.

7. Ibid., 171.

8. Ibid., 349.

9. For example, when Lyra is about to meet Mary Malone for the first time, the alethiometer tells her, "Do not lie to the Scholar." *The Subtle Knife*, 71.

10. Pullman, *The Amber Spyglass*, 461.

11. Ibid., 263.

Chapter 13: The Green Shoot

The authors' imaginative adaptation to begin the chapter is based on pages 355–357 of The Amber Spyglass.

1. From the FAQ page of Philip Pullman's official Web site; see http://www.philip-pullman.com/about_the_writing.asp.

2. These incidents are described in *The Golden Compass*, 259; *The Subtle Knife*, 34–35; *The Subtle Knife*, 276–277; *The Golden Compass*, 76; and *The Amber Spyglass*, 47.

3. See *The Amber Spyglass*, chapter 1, "The Enchanted Sleeper," 1–6.

4. Pullman, *The Amber Spyglass*, 362.

5. C. S. Lewis, *The Weight of Glory* (Grand Rapids, MI: William B. Eerdmans, 1972), 14–15.

6. Pullman, *The Amber Spyglass*, 362.

7. Ibid.

Chapter 14: Know Who It Is

The authors' imaginative adaptation to begin the chapter is based on pages 393–397 of The Amber Spyglass.

1. Pullman, *The Amber Spyglass*, 162.

2. Ibid., 209.

3. Burton Hatlen, "Pullman's *His Dark Materials*, A Challenge to the Fantasies of J. R. R. Tolkien and C. S. Lewis," in Lenz and Scott, *His Dark Materials Illuminated*, 76.

4. Pullman, *The Amber Spyglass*, 286.

5. Wendell W. Watters, "Christianity and Mental Health," *The Humanist*, November/December 1987, 32.

6. Anne-Marie Bird, "Circumventing the Grand Narrative: Dust as an Alternative Theological Vision in Pullman's *His Dark Materials*," in Lenz and Scott, *His Dark Materials Illuminated*, 189.

7. Pullman, *The Amber Spyglass*, 415.

8. It's worth mentioning that this is a bit hard to understand. Why attach this degree of "cosmic" significance to teenage sex? It isn't right and it isn't good, and it certainly isn't smart; but then it isn't particularly earth-shaking either—unless *your* child is the one who ends up with an unwanted pregnancy or a sexually transmitted disease.

9. Pullman, *The Amber Spyglass*, 394.

10. Milton, *Paradise Lost & Paradise Regained*, bk. 4, lines 741–743.

11. Pullman, *The Amber Spyglass*, 398.

12. "Mary, Alone," chapter 7 of *The Amber Spyglass*, 70–81.

Chapter 15: Eve

The authors' imaginative adaptation to begin the chapter is based on pages 408–417 of The Amber Spyglass.

1. Pullman, *The Golden Compass*, 271.

2. Pullman, *The Subtle Knife*, 244.

3. Ibid., 278.

4. Parker and Jones, *Dark Matters*, 149.

5. Milton, *Paradise Lost & Paradise Regained*, bk. 3, lines 99, 103–104.

Afterthoughts: The Missing Piece

1. Pullman, *The Subtle Knife*, 24.

2. See *The Amber Spyglass*, chapter 34, "There Is Now," 400–406.

3. Hatlen, in Lenz and Scott, 78. See also *The Amber Spyglass*, 325: "For us there is no elsewhere."

4. Ibid., 294.

5. Pullman, *The Golden Compass*, 102.

6. Ibid., 161.

7. Pullman, *The Amber Spyglass*, 344.

8. Watkins, *Dark Matter*, 21.

9. Ibid.

10. Andrew Leet, "Rediscovering Faith Through Science Fiction: Pullman's *His Dark Materials*," in Lenz and Scott, *His Dark Materials Illuminated*, 178.

11. Jean-Paul Sartre, *Being and Nothingness: An Essay on Phenomenological Ontology*, tran. H. Barnes (London: Methuen, 1957), 523.

12. Lenz and Scott, "Introduction," 10.

13. Pullman, *The Golden Compass*, 323.

14. Pullman, *The Subtle Knife*, 280 ff.

15. Pullman, *The Amber Spyglass*, 373.

16. Pullman, *The Golden Compass*, 104, 106.

17. Ibid., 107.

18. Pullman, *The Amber Spyglass*, 449.

19. Pullman, *The Golden Compass*, 107.

20. Watkins, *Dark Matter*, 31.

21. Ibid.

22. Pullman, *The Subtle Knife*, 13.

23. Pullman, *The Golden Compass*, 121.

24. Ibid., 119.

Bibliography

Blake, William. *The Poetry and Prose of William Blake*, edited by Geoffrey Keynes. New York: Random House, 1927.

Buber, Martin. *Good and Evil*, translated by Ronald Gregor Smith and Michael Bullock. Upper Saddle River, New Jersey: Prentice Hall, 1997.

_____. *I and Thou*, translated by Walter Kaufman. New York: Touchstone/Simon and Schuster, 1996.

Donne, John. *John Donne: Selected Poems*, edited by John Hayward. New York: Viking Penguin, 1950.

Gribbin, Mary, and John Gribbin. *The Science of Philip Pullman's His Dark Materials*. New York: Alfred A. Knopf, 2003.

Lenz, Millicent, and Carole Scott, eds. *His Dark Materials Illuminated: Critical Essays on Philip Pullman's Trilogy*. Detroit: Wayne State University Press, 2005.

Lewis, C. S. *The Discarded Image*. Cambridge: Cambridge University Press, 1994.

_____. *The Weight of Glory*. Grand Rapids, Michigan: William B. Eerdmans, 1972.

Milton, John. *Paradise Lost & Paradise Regained*, edited by Christopher Ricks. New York: Signet Classic, 2001.

MacDonald, George. *Discovering the Character of God*, edited by Michael R. Phillips. Minneapolis: Bethany House Publishers, 1989.

Parkin, Lance, and Mark Jones. *Dark Matters: An Unofficial and*

Unauthorised Guide to Philip Pullman's Internationally Bestselling His Dark Materials Trilogy. London: Virgin Books Ltd., 2005.

Pullman, Philip. *The Golden Compass.* New York: Random House, Inc., 1995.

_____. *The Subtle Knife.* New York: Random House, Inc., 1997.

_____. *The Amber Spyglass.* New York: Random House, Inc., 2000.

Rutland, Mark. *Behind the Glittering Mask.* Ann Arbor, Michigan: Servant Publications, 1996.

Sartre, Jean-Paul. *Being and Nothingness: An Essay on Phenomenological Ontology,* translated by H. Barnes. London: Methuen, 1957.

Tolkien, J. R. R. *The Tolkien Reader,* edited by Christopher Tolkien. New York: Ballantine Books, 1966.

Vitz, Paul. *Faith of the Fatherless.* Dallas: Spence, 1999.

Watkins, Tony. *Dark Matter: Shedding Light on Philip Pullman's Trilogy His Dark Materials.* Downers Grove, Illinois: InterVarsity Press, 2004.

From best-selling authors
KURT BRUNER and JIM WARE...